vibrant
simplicity

for my dear
Aunt Lucy,
with a heart
full of hope,
always!

lisalynnErica

L
i
s
a

L
y
n
n

E
r
i
c
s
o
n

P
o
e
t
r
y

book**Villages**

contents

preface

Do you hear whispers of hope on the darkest of days, or do life's challenges seem to taunt you like a cruel chant? When the stars do not align and the sun does not shine, what is your confidence, what is the source of your courage?

Any notion of valiance seems to pale in the face of the rigorous reality of life on this planet. Anyone who feels strong apparently suffers from a poetic naïveté, at best a victim of silly positivity, at worst a fool worth more harm than good. Life is hard, and no words or happy attitudes can make it any better.

Enough of that. Reality gets too much attention. Life is more than doom and gloom, and there is genuinely no need to wallow in despair. The solution, though, springs from a source beyond ourselves.

There is rhyme and reason in a posture of endless hope, a hope that never ends and that finds its ultimate fulfillment in God's presence. It is vibrant simplicity, a poetic pulse, a valiant song that pierces through the dismal landscape with everlasting love. It is as if our hearts already sense the tune and have been longing, for our entire existence, to simply hear the lyrics. Let us listen, let us sing.

a chain of love

The string of hearts,
A chain of love,
So pure and white,
As like a dove,
Like wispy clouds
Across the sky,
Flow free to form
Snow drifts up high,
As snowflake lace,
Chilled, crystal clear,
Like silky web
Reflects dew's tear,
This love which shines,
Connecting two,
A link of hearts,
From me to you.

31 Oct 1991

This is the first poem in one of my many handwritten notebooks, although I penned others as a child that are part of the larger collection.

beyond

Wide, upturned eyes behold
Ominous, burdened, lingering clouds,
Threats of torrential storm,
Yet the steady wind wipes grey away,
Unfolding golden rays set in boundless blue.
Beneath the darkness cast by laden clouds,
I know the sun shines behind the gloom.
Light beyond.

Pained, anguished eyes bemoan
A suspended, forsaken, lifeless Christ,
The collapse of apparent defeat,
Yet appointed triumph clears death away,
Promising lasting joy bought by precious
    blood.
Despite the suffering of the cross,
Christ knew the cause behind the price.
Love beyond.

Calm, earnest eyes befit
A solid, contented, surrendered core,
The strength of a believing heart,
Yet battles dare fight peace away,
Challenging ardent trust clad in armor bold.
Amid the struggles now in sight,
I know the victory and the hope.
Life beyond.

Feb-Mar 1997

"Blessed are those who have not seen and yet have believed." John 20:29b

"Now faith is confidence in what we hope for and assurance about what we do not see." Hebrews 11:1

cradled

I am cradled by the Child of the manger,
Who, though royal, left his throne for a
 rustic, humble scene,
Who, though reigning, left his glory so that
 he might intervene.
I owe homage to the King become a servant,
Who, though captive, offered freedom from
 the death of life on earth,
Who, though human, granted access to the
 God he was at birth.
I am singing to the Giver of my song,
Who, though far, yet is near, is the lyric of
 my praise,
Who, though God, yet has come, is
 Immanuel always.

3 Nov 1997

I developed the habit of writing poems for friends and
family to mark decisive moments and holidays. This
Christmas poem captures the incredible counterbalance of
the incarnate identity of Jesus.

darkness

Darkness extinguishes,
Shadows extend,
To dull the radiance and muffle the glow.
Eyes can't distinguish,
Only pretend
To sight the brightness his presence
    bestows.
Yet not defeated,
Yet not completed,
His power is intense,
His love is immense.
Life does still flourish,
Daylight returns,
To shine upon us and show us he's here.
Faith is now nourished,
And, believing, we yearn
To stand beside him who always is near.
Never retreated,
Never depleted,
His power is intense,
His love is immense.

Mar-Apr 1998

"He will be the sure foundation for your times, a rich store of salvation and wisdom and knowledge; the fear of the Lord is the key to this treasure." Isaiah 33:6

"Who among you fears the LORD and obeys the word of his servant? Let the one who walks in the dark, who has no light, trust in the name of the LORD and rely on their God."
Isaiah 50:10

"For we live by faith, not by sight." 2 Corinthians 5:7

seeking

In seeking, we find,
Searching, yearning, reaching toward
The Light, the End divine,
Granting, showing, being Lord.

When bright seems so dim,
Distant, endless, one path still
Leads on, points to him,
Constant, faithful, perfect will.

Hearts at rest, we wait,
Trusting, serving, hope alive—
Our God, his love innate,
Causes growth, makes us thrive.

15-16 Aug 1998

God is the ultimate answer to all of our unending yearnings.

i would speak

I would speak,
But words are frail,
Evading thoughts,
Which also fail.

Though my mind
Does try to know
My inclinations,
But they go.

Past my eyes,
Soaring, gone,
Through my view,
Then flitting on.

Recollections,
Hopes and dreams,
Beyond what I
Can grasp, it seems.

Fresh and vibrant,
Is this real?
What indeed
Is this I feel?

15-16 Aug 1998

The moment when a dream awakens is full of ardent marvel.

numbers 6

Oh, Lord, you bless me,
You keep me,
You make your face to shine upon me.
You're gracious to me, gracious to me,
You turn your face toward me,
You're gracious to me,
You turn your face toward me,
And give me peace.
Glory, glory in the highest,
Glory to Immanuel, my Savior.
God, you've come,
You dwell within me,
May I glorify your holy name.

Feb 1998

I spun the priestly blessing into a song of praise.

"The LORD bless you and keep you; the LORD make his face shine on you and be gracious to you; the LORD turn his face toward you and give you peace." Numbers 6:24-26

"Glory to God in the highest heaven, and on earth peace to those on whom his favor rests." Luke 2:14

sometimes

Sometimes the flowing only trickles,
Sometimes I thirst for one more drop.
When the waters cease to flood,
Nor blows a soothing wind,
Still, I wait, for you will come
And nourish me within.
Send a breeze, Lord,
Spirit's gentle touch,
May my fountains burst with joy,
For you have granted much.

You are God,
You are holy,
Glory to the one
Who is my only source.

Those days when my sparkle merely
    flickers,
Those days when I strain to find the light,
When the narrow way seems rough,
Or shadows mar my view,
Still, I wait, for you will come
And brighten me anew
Be my lamp, Lord,
Spirit's guiding flame,
May my path lead straight ahead,
I'm walking by your name.

You are God,
You are holy,
Glory to the one
Who is my only source.

And so I wait,
Strong and with courage,
With heart and mind and strength,
Loving you,
Loving you.

You are God,
You are holy,
I'm waiting for you now,
You are God.

16 Aug 1998

These are lyrics to a song I wrote, one that has lingered long and fervently in my spirit.

ever mindful

Ever mindful, ever speechless,
Ever thinking, without words.
Oh, to capture! Oh, to convey
The worth of this treasure,
Instead, I simply say,
"Aleluia!"
I could speak of vast immensity,
Of riches, luster, gold,
But phrases lack intensity
For this joy that I hold.
How to find a comparison,
An analogy that stands,
When the wonders I'm describing
Have been wrought by God's own hand?

Aleluia!
Such is the delight
Of living every moment
In the radiance of your light.
Aleluia!
Though I hardly can express
The measure of your beauty,
Of your deeds and faithfulness.

My efforts seem so meager,
But I'm convicted in my claim.
My heart is swelling, eager,
To glorify your name.

How to write a declaration,
An assertion true to you,
When my mental cogitations
Can't provide the praise you're due?

Aleluia!
Such is the delight
Of living every moment
In the radiance of your light.
Aleluia!
Though I hardly can express
The measure of your beauty,
Of your deeds and faithfulness.
Aleluia!
Aleluia to you, Lord!
Aleluia!

23 Aug 1998

This, too, is a song that depicts the sense of wonder and delight in my soul.

"Many, LORD my God, are the wonders you have done, the things you planned for us. None can compare with you; were I to speak and tell of your deeds, they would be too many to declare." Psalm 40:5

the heavens declare

The heavens declare it,
I join with them too.
They twinkle and rumble and pour forth for
    you,
The depth of your glory,
Splendor and scope.
I gaze on your beauty,
I focus with hope
On a God so tremendous,
Yet you're Father to me,
Reigning, majestic,
While close, intimately.

The skies do proclaim how
Your works are so grand,
Creating and tending
With your perfect hand.
The act of salvation,
Grace so complete,
Your presence is faithful,
And each need you meet.
You're a God so tremendous,
Yet you're Father to me,
Guiding and guarding,
Close, intimately.

In being and doing,
Oh, Father of mine,
May I be pleasing
To a God so divine.
The words of my mouth,
The core of my heart
I resign.

8 Sep 1998

This song bursts forth from within me when I glance at the skies.

"The heavens declare the glory of God; the skies proclaim the work of his hands. May these words of my mouth and this meditation of my heart be pleasing in your sight, LORD, my Rock and my Redeemer." Psalm 19:1, 14

journey

Journey, it's a journey I'm on,
Walking with abandon,
Quite unsure of the beyond.
Life is full, wonderfully complex,
My stride is steadied
By a God who knows what's next.

Even now,
There's a lilting deep within,
Even now,
There's a melody that echoes
Through the void of the unknown,
As I look ahead, not seeing,
But convinced I'm not alone.
Lord, You're good,
Good to me.
It's in Jesus that my fear can flee,
It's in Jesus that I'm free to sing.

Forward, I move onward every day,
Even in those moments
When the scene seems rather grey.
I press on with a God who stands secure—
By His power
I am sure I will endure.

Even now,
There's a lilting deep within,

Even now,
There's a melody that echoes
Through the void of the unknown,
As I look ahead, not seeing,
But convinced I'm not alone.
Lord, You're good,
Good to me.
It's in Jesus that my fear can flee,
It's in Jesus that I'm free to sing.

And so, I run the race,
Holding to the promise,
Like Abraham,
Hoping against hope,
Climbing every slope
By faith.

1-5 Dec 1998

I penned this song during a period of perplexity, trying to discover my path while determining to trust God when all was still unknown.

"Against all hope, Abraham in hope believed . . . he did not waver through unbelief regarding the promise of God, but was strengthened in his faith and gave glory to God, being fully persuaded that God had power to do what he had promised." Romans 4:18a, 20-21

our celebration

What compels our celebration?
A mere memory, a date?
Is our festive recollection
A tradition we create?

Manger, stable, shepherds, wise men,
All a scene from long ago,
Now depicted amid the flurry
Of a season pagans know.

As we honor Christ's arrival,
A historic, grand event,
May we also tell the wonders
Which his purposed birth has meant.

God among us is the marvel,
The Messiah come as man,
Who in living and in dying,
Gave a life no other can.

Thus convinced we utter boldly
Who this Christ is even now—
He who entered and departed
Still deserves our reverent bow.

2 Dec 1998, New York City

This poem is part of the holiday collection, penned over a period of many years. I happened to be visiting my brother in NY when I wrote this one.

not a fraying

Not a fraying at the hemline,
Nor a knife to split the weave,
Cut the curtain that required
That which man could not achieve,

But, instead, a downward ripping,
Threads dividing, fabric torn,
From above, an entrance granted,
A communion now reborn,

An unveiling most revealing
As God cast away our sin,
For his death displays the nature
Of the God he's always been:

Ever loving, reaching toward us,
Ever strong, with mighty hand,
Which, extended, guides the holy,
Who by faith in him can stand.

21 Mar 1999, Quinta do Conventinho, Portugal

I wrote this Easter-themed poem at one of my favorite
poetic places, an enchanting 16th century convent that
eventually became a museum not far from my home in
Póvoa de Santo Adrião, Portugal.

"At that moment the curtain of the temple was torn in two
from top to bottom." Matthew 27:51

"One thing God has spoken, two things I have heard: 'Power belongs to you, God, and with you, Lord, is unfailing love.'" Psalm 62:11-12a

in you

In you, Jesus,
I am whole,
I am holy.
May my heart
Be wholehearted,
And in living may I show
The abundance you bestow,
So that others then will know
This life.
Resting in you, Jesus,
By faith I am complete.
My existence is to serve you,
And to linger at your feet.
So I love to love what you love,
As I cling unto the vine,
Bearing fruit that bears you glory
With this life that is not mine.

16 Aug 1999

I have sung this poem so many times as a prayer.

when i draw near

When I draw near,
I see you are here.
If only I'd looked before.
In a world insecure,
You always are sure,
And ready to love me more.
Timelessness surrounds you,
Forever and right now.
Your countless ways astound me,
Your presence speaks of how
You never shift or waver,
Sleep or turn away.
You cast your faithful favor
On the ones who walk your way.
So, I worship you, God,
You're here to hear my song.
I wonder in your closeness,
You're beside me all along.
Keep me looking to you, Jesus,
Guard my heart from disarray,
That in fervor and in firmness
I'll behold you every day.

19 Aug 1999

This poem pulses with my perspective on life and is a song
that I keep singing.

peering

Peer upon the dim, stark setting
At the dingy, earthy site,
And behold this tender, meek one,
Such a tiny, fragile sight.

Feel the crudeness of the cradle,
Manger rough, repulsing touch,
Textures wild, piercing, scratching,
Harsh surroundings wanting much.

Breathe the air, its staleness heavy,
Smells befitting beasts and sod,
Wafting scents, aromas reeking,
Fragrances, their perfumes odd.

Listen closely to the quiet
As the Word lets out a sound,
Not a grand, incisive statement,
Baby's cry, not yet profound.

Speak the Truth of who this Life is,
How the Way leads us to sing.
Silence bursts with prancing echoes,
Voices chorus, heralding
The Messiah's entering.
Each sense in tune, a birth observed,
So opportune, love undeserved.

Oh, taste and see, regard Christ still,
Embrace how he came of his will.

5 Oct 1999

This poem is part of the holiday series, pulling all of the senses into the nativity picture.

where green overflows

Where green overflows
In life's lush abundance,
Each tendril by tending refined,
To silence inclined,
I soak up the quiet
And the hush this hiatus well knows.

But promptly a voice,
All stillness discarding,
As sun dissipating the dew,
No solace now due,
My name softly spoken,
In his knowledge I fully rejoice.

I pause at the sound,
As garden becomes meadow,
My Shepherd, I follow the Word,
A sheep who has heard,
A branch on the vine,
By his call, his fresh pasture I've found.

5-6 Feb 2000

"He asked her, 'Woman, why are you crying? Who is it you
are looking for?'
   Thinking he was the gardener, she said, 'Sir, if you have
carried him away, tell me where you have put him, and I
will get him.' Jesus said to her, 'Mary.' She turned toward
him and cried out in Aramaic, 'Rabboni!' (which means
'Teacher')." John 20:15-16

sing in the shadow

I will sing in the shadow,
In the shelter of your wings
I will soar,
I will be restored.
When I'm wearied by my striving,
Teary, torn and tired,
I set my heart on pilgrimage,
It's your presence I desire.
In looking up, not inward,
I worship, walk and wait.
This righteousness is resting
By faith, not in my gait.
You are a sun and a shield,
You cover me, and it's revealed
That hiding means freedom,
Dependence is power,
The poor ones own your kingdom,
And pride will only cower.
Oh, refuge, Oh, God of boundless might,
Oh, revival when my spirit is contrite,
Turn my sighing into flying,
My struggle into strength.
As I hope in you my feathers flutter,
And my running conquers length.
I will sing in the shadow,
In the shelter of your wings
I will soar,

I will be restored,
Evermore.

30 Mar 2000

This poem is a song of praise that my heart still sings.

"Because you are my help, I sing in the shadow of your wings." Psalm 63:7

dawn to dusk

From dawn to dusk,
All dark dispelling,
I live as a child of light,
In time of trouble,
Tightly dwelling.
Oh, Lord, it's in you I delight.
Upheld within your hand,
I inherit the land.
In plenty and peace, I reside,
Safe in your salvation,
Your promised protection,
The pasture you richly provide.

Make my steps firm, Lord.
Though I stumble, I'll not fall.
Forever my foothold,
My fretting you forestall.
Shining like the noonday sun,
Defining my days by what you've done,
In the way of wisdom,
In you I overcome.

A life of love,
The law of living.
I'm looking to please you, Oh, Lord,
Your fruit and fragrance
Freely giving
A flourishing, ground unexplored.

In your refuge I rest,
Your truth I attest.
Your goodness grows greater than grass.
The faithful not forsaken,
In trusting I'm taken
To stillness no schemes can surpass.

Make my steps firm, Lord.
Though I stumble, I'll not fall.
Forever my foothold,
My fretting you forestall.
Shining like the noonday sun,
Defining my days by what you've done,
In the way of wisdom,
In you I overcome.

8-9 Jun 2000

This song is based on Psalm 37 and Ephesians 5:1-17,
surging with light and love.

honey

Honey
Drizzled delicacy,
Golden goodness,
Nectar nourishing me,
Savored syrup,
Sugary swirl,
Yet my palate's pleasure
No flavor will unfurl,
Like the feast that I've found,
The abundance of affection,
Pure and plentiful, profound,
I revel in reflection.

I will never taste
Another love as sweet,
I will never know
Compassion so complete.
It is long and wide
And deep and high,
I'm the bride
You satisfy.
For my heart,
All cares aside,
There is no counterpart.

Water,
Rushing ripples or rills,
Lapping liquid,

On my drought it distills.
Sprinkled shower,
Dryness now drenched,
Yet my tongue is tickled,
And my craving is quenched
By delights as I drink
From a fountain flowing, filling,
Thirst forgotten as I think,
This spring in me is spilling.

I will never taste
Another love as sweet,
I will never know
Compassion so complete.
It is long and wide
And deep and high,
I'm the bride
You satisfy.
For my heart,
All cares aside,
There is no counterpart.
For my heart,
There is no counterpart.

25-28 Jun 2000

"How sweet are your words to my taste, sweeter than honey to my mouth!" Psalm 119:103

strong song

I'm strong by his presence,
Sufficient, replete,
A wisdom all-knowing,
A power complete.
My Savior, a baby,
Almighty, a man.
The fool cannot fathom
His life-giving plan.

I'm singing his praises,
His sovereign design
Responds to my weakness,
My heart I incline.
As trusting, triumphant,
I marvel headlong
At Jesus, the theme
Of my victory song.

11 Aug 2000

By summertime, I was already thinking about the upcoming
Christmas holiday season, poised with a poem to mark the
moment.

ever looking

Ever looking,
Penetrating,
Probing the terrain,
Sweeping, scanning,
Searching but in vain,

For the living,
Breath that beckons,
Brims with bounty's gale,
Rushes, reckons
Reason only stale,

In the lifeless,
Dull deception,
Deadly masquerade,
Foolish fiction,
Futile pageant played,

When our longing,
Purest passion,
Pleasure out of reach,
Free of fashion,
Fullness all beseech,

Has been lifted,
Burden broken,
Bolsters earnest eyes,

Strongly spoken,
Silencing the lies.

Surge is stifled,
Rest is rifled,
Horizon bleak,
Hopeless peaks,
But still he speaks,
A stunning summons,
Bidding all belief:
The soul who seeks
A lasting lifeline
Reaches in relief.

Feb 2001

Ever looking. For the living. In the lifeless. When our longing. Has been lifted.

"You study the Scriptures diligently because you think that in them you have eternal life. These are the very Scriptures that testify about me, yet you refuse to come to me to have life." John 5:39-40

if only

If only I could chirp so chipperly and with
   intent,
If only I could tweet and tell you what my
   mind has meant.
My heart wants to hum,
My soul wants to strum.
The birds begin at daybreak
And chatter all along.
In cheerful chant I chorus
And burst into this song.
Oh, the joy as I join them,
Letting lips lift up your name!
Sovereign Lord,
In chime and chord,
This sound is for your fame.

You who spread out the earth,
You who stretched out the sky,
Yours the wonderful worth.
For your sake, you supply
All my breath,
Till my death,
And beyond:
Blessed life, loving bond.

If only we would cling more closely
To your holding hand,
If only we would toss our trinkets,

Pettiness we've planned.
We forfeit your grace,
We glimpse not your face.
The sustenance of sparrows
You send forth from your store,
In Christ your kindness keeps us
And strengthens us to soar.
Oh, your call of compassion!
We're so slow and shy to shout!
Almighty God,
I pulse, not plod,
To speak your praise, sing out.

You who spread out the earth,
You who stretched out the sky,
Yours the wonderful worth.
For your sake, you supply
All my breath,
Till my death,
And beyond:
Blessed life, loving bond.

My Redeemer,
Your splendor sparks my voice.
Your renown is
The reason I rejoice.
For your sake, you supply
All my breath,
Till my death,
And beyond:

Blessed life, loving bond.
I respond.

19-20 May 2001

This poem is a song that springs from two passages.

"The birds of the sky nest by the waters; they sing among the branches." Psalm 104:12

"Sing to the LORD a new song, his praise from the ends of the earth." Isaiah 42:10

luke: a version in verse

Rising, the sun
Of rescue, redemption,
In mercy extended,
A righteousness done.

Peace now, the sight,
As promised by prophets:
This marvelous entrance,
A pathway, a light.

Straightened and smoothed,
Salvation from shadows:
Messiah's endowment,
As, shining, he soothed.

Help sent and shown
To hungry and humble,
By mighty enabling,
A holiness sown.

Fearing, we serve
In freedom, forgiven,
And made to extol him
Whose face we'll observe.

Gladly, he still
Gives goodness and guidance.

The Most High is ever,
In glory, our fill.

9-11 Aug 2001

This poem is based on Luke 1:46-79, pondering the joyful
path that Jesus opened upon his birth.

meager measures

Meager measures,
Transient treasures,
Merriment that's mustered, tried.
Season stilted,
Wishes wilted,
Sensing something wanting, wide.

Gaping, garbled,
Marshy, marbled,
Giving, getting, more, galore.
Scamper, scurry,
Festive flurry,
Sentiments both fall and soar.

Yet our yearning,
Urge upturning,
Yule's unyielding undertow,
Surges, steady,
Endless eddy,
Scours each scenario.

For the focus,
Living locus,
Full and lasting, limit-free,
Sure, sustaining,
Aimed, attaining,
Still surpasses all we see.

9 Jan 2002

"So we fix our eyes not on what is seen, but on what is unseen, since what is seen is temporary, but what is unseen is eternal." 2 Corinthians 4:18

remove the dross

Remove the dross, the glaring gloss,
The wretched, wasteful layer,
The sins that haunt, the sheen I flaunt,
The flaws that I repair.
Reshape, remold, omit the old.
I'm cast upon your care,
My crust now drilled, my cracks now filled,
This fragile earthenware.
Oh, Craftsman, I've aspired
To be what you desire, to do what you
    require,
Yet swollen striving crush aside—
Oh, crumble all my pride.
Remove the dross, the glaring gloss—
May your mastery preside.

9 Sep 2005

My alma mater, Wheaton College, asked me to write a
text for a daily devotional book, *Stones of Remembrance
2: Wheaton's Living Stones,* published in 2006. My entry,
which appeared on the January 9 page, included a reflective
portion of prose probing the topic of self-righteousness,
along with this poem.

"Yet you, LORD, are our Father. We are the clay, you are the
potter; we are all the work of your hand." Isaiah 64:8

writer's psalm

The Lord is the literary master,
No annals nor linguistics I lack.
His passages lead me to mental repose,
His phrases guide me to mindful reflection.
He enlivens my being.
He moves me to right thinking and doing
    for his endless renown.
If I begin to tread in sinuous depths, I fear
    no darkness,
For your text summons me,
Your concepts and corrections prod me to
    steady turf.
Your bounty nourishes me with truth in the
    midst of famine,
You consecrate me to yourself by the
    breath of your mouth.
Certainly, your revealed goodness and grace
    are ever at my fingertips,
And I will reside with your word in one
    continuous chapter.

23 Oct 2011

This is a poet's rendition of Psalm 23.

thanks declared

Unaware,
In silence and stride,
That my course and his
Would abruptly collide.
Unimpaired,
In purposed pursuit,
Ran he who would pluck
This his prey absolute.
Now ensnared,
My flesh fearing harm,
I hollered to God,
Who all foes can disarm.
My despair,
With mercy was met,
A rescue with care,
That my crisis offset.
Once spared,
I soon thanked the one
God sent alongside,
Yet it's thanks just begun.
Well aware,
My gratitude turns,
Unfettered, to God,
It's for him my heart yearns.

3 Jan 2012

"I love the LORD, for he heard my voice; he heard my cry for mercy. Because he turned his ear to me, I will call on him as long as I live." Psalm 116:1-2

On the morning of November 16, 2011, I was walking in a quiet neighborhood in Lancaster, PA, when suddenly I noticed a man running behind me, then racing toward me. He was not another jogger, he was a crazed chaser, intent on assaulting me. His glare was wild. He wielded two impromptu implements as weapons and brusquely ordered me to hold onto the pole of a nearby speed limit sign. As I did, he paced back and forth, developing his plan. I stood frozen but clear-minded, and I decided to deliberately say something that I knew had the potential to be controversial. I yelled, "Jesus, save me!" At that, the man continued on the prowl, near me but never touching me. Meanwhile, a neighbor man, driving by on his way to work, noticed the crisis and lingered, cruising up and down the street while calling the police. In the intervening minutes, the assaulter ran back to his home, just around the corner. The police arrived, arrested the perpetrator and drove me back to my apartment. I had been spared.

flux

Only seashells,
Iridescent,
Hints of luster, now strewn,
And some seaweed,
Reminiscent,
Limp and pungent, so soon.

Once in movement,
Buoyant, quickened,
Deeply swimming at sea,
Then moored, surfless,
Saline, thickened,
Sandy, sodden debris.

Undercurrent,
In subsiding,
Softly mournful, exhales,
Chiding gently,
And confiding,
As its egress entails.

Tidal pattern,
Grief in motion,
This receding would seem,
Pulling, tugging,
To the ocean,
Where all resources teem.

Now abruptly,
Here arises,
Fluent wellspring, ashore,
Yet another
Wave surprises,
Foaming, splashing, with more.

4 May 2012

"Out of his fullness we have all received grace in place of grace already given." John 1:16

I have had so many situations in my life when a beautiful, brimming experience slips away before I have hardly savored it. Time after time, I am faced with a reluctant goodbye. As a result, I have learned to trust that God will bring another good experience to replace what is gone. I have come to see it as waves on the shoreline—one bit of grace after another, in and out. The sorrow of the goodbye is sweetened by the hope of an endless flow. Grace, on and on.

this tear

I'm not ashamed to let this tear
Slide boldly down my skin,
To know its source,
With no remorse
For sentiments within.

Oh, salty stream, release this ache,
The remnant now so sore,
Flood through my sighs
And soothe the whys,
When I'm still wanting more.

I will allow my heart to speak,
Not muffled by my mind,
To recognize
And not disguise
The way I am inclined.

My deepest voice I vocalize,
Unhindered, without fear,
And fully face,
Even embrace,
While feeling every tear.

8 Sep 2012

"Listen to my words, LORD, consider my lament. Hear my
cry for help, my King and my God, for to you I pray. In the
morning, LORD, you hear my voice; in the morning I lay my
requests before you and wait expectantly." Psalm 5:1-3

when urges are stifled

When urges are stifled in a pious
    masquerade,
And feelings, though worthy, dismissed,
A dream that was swelling is slowly left to
    fade,
A cheek needing contact, unkissed.

When scrutiny squelches a word that would
    be said,
And milder expressions lack grit,
An edited statement now languishes
    instead,
Though thoughts deep within still don't
    quit.

When sentences packaged by norms seem
    stiff and cold,
Deception meanders around,
And platitudes violate truth that's raw and
    bold,
While treasures concealed stay unfound.

When honor becomes a distorted obstacle,
Diminished existence results.
Concern for what's right warps into a
    spectacle,
And freedom to thrive it insults.

Why squander opportunities when we can live
In vibrant engagement that's real,
Composing a genuine, honest narrative,
Authentic, with unashamed zeal?

21 Jan 2013

When we force our thoughts, feelings, words and actions through the filter of what we think is right or appropriate, we often make the wrong decision, opting for restraint. The result is that we deceive ourselves and others, repressing honesty and replacing it with a hindered language and lifestyle. We long for a vigorous, vibrant simplicity, but we settle for what we assume is safer—yet is actually dangerous.

celebrate the silence

I'll celebrate the silence,
This hush that smothers sounds,
A symphony suspended,
As quietness surrounds.

This calm is not idyllic,
Its restless, noiseless shout
Now tauntingly invades me
And tries to summon doubt.

When merriment is muffled,
And laughter slumbers long,
I'd rather craft some clamor
Or rush to sing a song.

And yet, perhaps this nothing
Is everything I need,
This stanza with no lyric,
An emptiness to heed.

I wait, though not an echo
Reverberates right now.
This void, its starkness aching,
Still has a voice somehow.

I'll listen to this language,
My eagerness controlled,

With heart still pulsing, steady,
And let this lull unfold.

2 Feb 2013

"When times are good, be happy; but when times are bad,
consider this: God has made the one as well as the other.
Therefore, no one can discover anything about their future."
Ecclesiastes 7:14

If I claim to embrace every moment as it unfolds, with
a sense of wonder, steadied by confidence in God's
sovereignty, then I must be consistent. I must include in
my embrace the periods of silence that God imposes and
wait upon him patiently. When the scenario is perplexing or
painful, this too I must accept with open arms. I have been
prodding myself to do that, whether circumstances are
sparkling or sorrowful.

studio in disguise

A studio in disguise,
Where phrases resolve,
And palettes evolve.
A workshop under the skies,
Organic displays
The artist conveys.

The poet her muse refines,
And finds in a tree
An apt simile.
Each creature the space enshrines,
A painter's brush strokes,
And piper invokes,

As landscape becomes a host
For crafts now inspired
By wonders admired.
Together and yet engrossed
In meadow and pond,
Or glimpses beyond.

In solitude, now combined,
To savor and share,
Perhaps unaware,
As God, who all this designed,
Sees more than the views:
Our being renews.

15 Feb 2013

I had passed local artist Suk Shuglie many times while out walking, but on that particular Sunday at Overlook Park, we stopped and spoke longer. I learned of her artistry, and we confided in each other that the setting serves as inspiration and context for her painting as well as my writing. She invited me to her gallery, and we parted ways. Shortly afterward, that same afternoon in the park, curiously, a man retrieved a bagpipe from his car and, walking along the pathway under a wide open sky, proceeded to play. I was struck by the bond between the three of us, each of us responding to our Creator in his arena, yearning to share our resulting art.

tangible

Limbs extended, muscles flexed,
Grasping for what I want next.
Earnest the pose,
So I suppose—
Such is the rhythm I chose.

Words repeated, pious chant,
Not with sly or crafty slant—
What is your will?
Come and fulfill,
While I am speaking and still.

Yet perhaps I say too much,
In my longing for your touch.
Though I'm sincere,
I need to hear,
Listening as I draw near.

This inversion places me
In contrite humility,
Just letting go,
For I don't know
What you will wisely bestow.

Tangible results you've sent,
While I seek, with posture bent,
Not for my bliss,

Or goals amiss,
But for your glory in this.

4 May 2013

It was the morning after the National Day of Prayer, and I was pondering with two other people the practice and effect of prayer. We considered that, rather than employ so many words, we would do well to listen more. And one of my companions challenged us with the concept that genuine prayer produces tangible results and glorifies God.

this is not hell

This is not hell—
The roses still smell,
And butterflies
Would not tell me lies.
To flower they flutter—
I struggle and sputter,
And see them take flight,
And wish that I might,
But here I am, grounded,
Hunched, hurting, confounded,
Just thinking of thorns
And all that adorns
My lot of decay,
This plot where my play
Is masking pain,
So others see joy—
It's all in vain—
These roses annoy:
They waft toward my sorrow,
Their fragrance I borrow—
I can't resist
Their scent—they insist
That life hasn't died,
Despite what's implied
By all this despair
That smothers the air,
For butterflies soar,
And blossoms say more:

A whisper, a shout,
Defying my doubt
That what I claim
Is flourishing still,
While hellish flame
Now threatens to kill,
And suffocates hope
As I merely cope.
And yet there are roses—
Their presence imposes—
They prompt me, they prod,
My senses breathe life,
While butterflies nod
At wallowing strife
To just not recoil,
As if burning,
But rise from the soil
In my yearning.

6 Oct 2014

Autumn had arrived somewhat abruptly, with leaves
falling from the trees and an unexpected chill in the air.
Simultaneously, I knew someone who was facing another
kind of deterioration, in an agonizing form. One day,
as I passed a rosebush that still held some blossoms,
I bent over to smell the flowers. Such a sweet aroma.
Immediately, the thought came to my mind, "This is not
hell—the roses still smell." And the poem poured forth from
there.

the broken one

The broken one loves me,
And I love furthermore
Every piece of his story,
Every shard on the floor,
That is tarnished and weathered,
And the tempests have bettered
How they blend in their hues—
Stone and stone,
Tone on tone—
Though I cannot confuse
A mosaic of beauty
With the pain in the art,
While it was not his duty
To design every part—
All I know is his heart
Isn't broken forever,
And the hurts cannot sever
All the love there within,
Even though it has been
Shard and shard,
Hard as hard,
That he cannot control—
An affront to his soul,
Yet his love—it is whole,
And within its design
Is a heart—it is mine—
I am broken as well,

Into pieces and grit,
And the places they fell
Are a beautiful fit,
For when broken ones bond—
Speck and speck,
Fleck on fleck—
Art makes love, and beyond
Every fragment and grain,
Every crack, every pain,
That no soul can sustain
When it throbbingly aches—
That's when love comes along,
In between all the breaks,
Making everything hold:
A mosaic—behold—
It's a pattern we share,
All the pieces laid bare,
And our love is right there.

14 Feb 2016

The broken one. The beautiful mosaic.

promise spoken

The promise was spoken,
So why am I broken,
Not really by doubt,
Just figuring out
How it will be kept?
I pick it to pieces,
But it's not my thesis,
For it is his word,
Which now I have heard
And know he's adept
At always fulfilling
And never once spilling
His word in the dirt,
Yet I am alert,
And quickly I ask
What is his intention,
As if his invention
Were mine to know how,
Right here and right now,
But it's not my task.
Then, lovingly scolding
And gently withholding,
He tells me to trust—
And trust him I must—
For that is my part,
While his is the doing,
The promised pursuing
Of what he has said,

And he wants instead
This only: my heart.

20 Feb 2016

He promised, and I trusted. Why, then, did I ask how he was going to accomplish what he had promised? That is not for me to know.

love in disguise

There's love on display,
Disguised as mere play,
But sometimes the heart
Is falling apart,
As frolic is feigned,
And pleasure is pained
By scavenging wrongs,
Like pestering songs
That seem to attack,
Yet love can fight back.
With blood on its hands,
From far-away lands,
For Jesus shed life
And settled the strife—
He rose above death,
With bolstering breath.
His bellowing love
Still hovers above,
Around, and inside
The struggles we hide.
When life takes a hit
Love still has the grit
To play, and play hard—
Unbeaten, unmarred.
Our love has its source
In his, and of course,
We cannot despise
Its bloody disguise.

When playing is done,
Love's only begun
To love even more—
That's what life is for.

08 May 2016

True love suffers and sacrifices, traversing the territory of
life's struggles with unbeaten tenacity.

poems full of tears

Cascading through the centuries,
And spilling through the years,
They dampen all our memories,
These poems full of tears.
They swell the parchment,
Smudge the scroll,
And languish with a sigh,
They groan for a romantic goal
That seems to swerve and die,
Or others moan with deadly grief
That mocks the joy of birth—
Each poet's pen finds no relief
While circling the earth.
As such I catalog them all,
They all seem so the same—
In all I've read, I can't recall
A poem I could name.
Well, that was until yesterday,
And now the poem's mine:
My daughter came to me to say,
"Um, Daddy, I'm not fine.
My heart is crying, can you hear
The whimper from inside?
Come close to me, come close, be near—
I'll tell you what I hide.
I look at all my friends around,
The father-daughter pairs,

And how I hurt is so profound—
My life is not like theirs.
No, Daddy, I don't blame you, no—
I know your love is real—
I only wanted you to know
That this is how I feel."
That's what she said, and now I write,
Through wet and teary eyes,
And now I know the poet's plight,
While blotting my own cries.

9 Oct 2016

Broken families blot tender tears that the rest of the world
rarely sees.

god has not failed us

"God has not failed us,
Nor will he ever,"
That's what he said.
Life can assail us,
Hauntingly clever,
But we're not dead,
And yet I feel victimized
By my mind,
Seeing all goodness disguised
And unkind.

Hope is elusive,
Empty and ghostly,
Teasing my dreams,
While I'm reclusive,
Somnolent mostly,
And so, it seems,
This is an awful nightmare—
I can't rest—
While evil eyes only stare,
All in jest.

But as I'm sinking
Deeper and dying,
Age-old advice
Comes to my thinking,
Pleading and vying,

And I think twice,
Telling the enemy: "No,
God's not gone."
Telling my mind what I know,
I press on.

24 Nov 2016

I heard a man say, with conviction, "God has not failed us, nor will he ever." And, as another friend tells me with a cautionary tone, the mind is man's greatest enemy. We must bear the former confidence and battle the latter foe.

segregation v. love

I had a dream,
A dream of a day
When, well, I won't say.
It might all seem
Just nonsense to you,
And I wish I knew
How to turn
These wrongs into right—
There's black and there's white,
While I yearn
To swiftly erase
The lines set in place.
But I'm here,
I'm on the wrong side,
And it's clear
This dream that I hide
Is hidden so well,
It's gone from my speech—
From here I can tell
It's just out of reach.
It's pointless to try,
I secretly cry.
But then you say,
"Take courage, be strong!
It's not cliché—
There's hope for this wrong.
Go rescue the ones who can't speak,
Whom you love.

You're stronger than this, you're not weak. God above
Is with you in this—
He knows the despair,
The blight without bliss—
Go, show them you care."
I hear you and think,
"I'll keep that in mind,
But I'd rather sink
And slowly unwind."
Then last night I slept—
Well, I couldn't sleep—
I laughed and I wept
And thought how to keep
My dream still alive.
Your words were my muse—
They came to revive
Me, and I refuse
To quit in my quest—
I'll do as you said, and then,
With courage attest:
Now I have a dream, again.

15 Jan 2017

On the surface, this may seem to be about segregation, but it's actually about being separated from the ones you love. Love is stronger than any black/white barrier. If it is Segregation v. Love, love wins, case closed. Take courage!

"Speak up for those who cannot speak for themselves, for the rights of all who are destitute. Speak up and judge fairly; defend the rights of the poor and needy." Proverbs 31:8-9

how am i?

How am I, you ask.
I just breathed again,
And so, I'm alive.
It's no easy task,
This living, and then
You prod me to thrive,
To make of this life something more,
But what is this day really for?

I breathe in and out,
It comes and it goes,
Like all that I've lost,
While I have no doubt
That no one else knows
The stifling cost
Of what my existence requires,
And yet, your one question inspires.

How am I? You know.
I'm here—that's enough—
It's all I can do.
I breathe as I go,
And slog through my stuff—
I've shared it with you.
And knowing you know and you care,
I breathe, as I breathe in the air.

22 Jan 2017

I imagine the thoughts of someone who has lost so much
and who hardly knows how to answer the simple question:
"How are you?"

no words

God spoke and it was so—
A word or two or three—
And life took the cue.
Well, I'm not God, I know,
And there's no word in me
To speak and to do
The things that God does,
But listen because

My silence is my voice
That speaks when I'm in pain,
With nothing to say.
I see no other choice,
And languages are vain
When life hurts this way,
And so, I don't speak
When I'm feeling weak.

I'm weak, and yet I'm strong,
For I know deep within
That, even in this,
You hear my silent song—
The drumbeat and the din,
When life isn't bliss—
And quietly care,
When words are not there.

20 May 2017

A friend was grappling with life's grit and said to me gently:
"I really don't want to talk anymore. Please understand. Just
be quiet."

this shadow of death

This shadow of death
Has taken my breath
Away, and with each step I pant.
It's dusty and dry,
I shuffle and sigh,
And wish I could stop, but I can't.

I can't stop—not yet—
I'd only regret
If I were to sink in despair.
The shadows allure,
And I see no cure,
But only this deathly, dark stare.

The quiet just jeers,
And mocks all my fears,
The monsters that lurk in my mind.
As grey turns to black,
In stealthy attack,
This darkness is making me blind.

It's quite an abyss,
But whoa, now—what's this?
A prodding from out of the blue.
So I step aside,
And see now the wide
And cavernous cliff in my view.

I almost fell in,
But something akin
To kindness prevented my fall.
It felt like a rod,
Its comfort seemed odd,
Like something I strangely recall.

It's psalm twenty-three:
The sheep—that is me,
The valley, a harrowing pit.
I'm hopeless at best—
My bruises attest
To how I am clearly unfit.

That's life as a sheep,
And I cannot keep
Myself in this dark that can kill,
And so now I must
Find someone to trust,
Who knows every rock, every rill.

I want not, I need
Just Jesus to lead,
Just like he did moments ago.
From darkness to dawn,
He'll guide, on and on—
His goodness and mercy I'll know.

18 Jun 2017

Psalm 23 delves into the depths, where the shadow of death lurks over our lives. I read this poem to my dear friend Terri Roberts on my last visit to her before she took her final breath.

i am beat

I am beat,
And that's really all to say—
That's the story of my day.
This defeat
Is the worst that I could score,
Though I tried for so much more,
But there is no way to win—
Let me tell you how it's been.

Pushed aside
By the one who wants me out—
I can't win, I have no doubt.
Yes, I've tried,
For I am a man of peace,
But this turmoil just won't cease—
It's no game, and it's no fight—
There's no way to make it right.

I am done,
But I didn't lose my heart,
And the end is just the start.
I've begun
To discover that I can
Still live fully as a man,
Who is very much alive,
And wholeheartedly can thrive.

What I lost
Didn't rob me of my soul—
That is something no one stole—
And the cost
Is another part of me,
Deep inside that none can see.
This defeat I pay with pain,
But I didn't love in vain.

I have learned
That with love there is a price—
Nothing ever will suffice.
I have turned
This defeat into a life,
Where I love despite the strife,
With the strength from God above,
For the greatest thing is love.

25 Dec 2017 / 7 Jan 2018

I know someone who has been stripped of all apparent
honor and who yet persists with an honorable posture of
love.

i hate my life

I heard what you said,
The downcast announcement
You spoke with a sigh,
That barely was heard.
You can't see ahead,
And this sad pronouncement
Is only a lie
That tricks you, absurd,
So, don't say it—"I hate my life"—
There's more to all this than your strife.

I watch you each day,
The endless compassion
Of such a great man,
So wise and so strong,
And there is no way
That all of your passion
Is nothing more than
A meaningless song,
So, don't hate your life when it's tough—
Your value is more than enough.

Don't hate what is now—
Your life is a treasure,
A platinum joy
That multiplies more.
You cannot see how
The pain and the pleasure

Since you were a boy,
It all came before,
And made you the man that I know—
I love you, and let it be so.

22 Nov 2018

Sometimes an immigrant reaches the point where they
only feel like making this pronouncement: "I hate my life."
And yet, perhaps all that they lack is the assurance of being
loved.

customs

No, nothing to declare,
For them to know.
I've traveled everywhere,
And as I go,
There's nothing I can tell,
At least not very well,
About the big and small things that I've
    packed.
My customs declaration is a fact.

There's nothing they could see,
If they would try.
It's all inside of me—
I'll tell you why.
I'm not quite what I was,
And that is all because
Of big and small things all along the way,
And there is one more thing for me to say.

There's something that I hide,
I will admit.
I carried it inside—
It barely fit—
The love I have for you,
That grows in all I do,
But as I went through customs, I was
    clear—
They couldn't see my heart, and I am here!

23 Dec 2018

I often feel as if I am hiding something when I claim that I have nothing to declare while going through the customs clearance at airports. I gain so much when I travel that, although intangible, is a great value worth announcing.

about the new year

I won't say a thing
About the new year—
That didn't start yet,
And nor will I sing,
"There's nothing to fear!"
So I won't regret
That I have composed just a lie,
So, listen, and I'll tell you why.

I think and I feel,
As I look ahead
At all of the days,
That fear is so real,
And joy could be dead,
A frightening daze,
Where all of life's dreams fall apart
And anguish takes over the heart.

But that is not how
The story will be—
The fear will not win—
I know that right now,
So, listen to me,
And I will begin:
There's much we could fear, but fear not,
For fearing can't conquer a lot.

The year may be new,
But what is not old
Is what we both know:
Our God can see through
All that will unfold,
And this much is true—
With God and in love we are strong,
And such is our fearlessness song!

30 Dec 2018

It is so common and so trite to make claims that the New Year will be terrific. We do not know the future, and yet, we do know that God leads us forward, always in love.

life also ends

Life also ends,
When what had begun
Is breathing no more.
Fate somehow sends
A day to be done,
And legend and lore
Have tried through the ages to tell
The story we all know so well.

The tale is true,
That there is a day
When life becomes death.
Now it is you,
And there is no way
To capture your breath.
I watch as you slowly exhale,
And suddenly life seems so pale.

Fairytales try
To end happily,
But now this is real.
I see you die,
And there is no glee,
Except that I feel
That somehow the end is a start,
With all of your love in my heart.

23 Jun 2019

My friend traveled over 600 miles by car to visit his father, whom he had not been able to see in many years. However, the encounter never happened because his father suddenly had to leave town due to a death in the family. When I expressed my sorrow that the long-awaited visit never happened, my friend said, soberly and with an air of acceptance, "Life also ends."

challenged

I'm challenged in my mind—
There's nothing in my brain,
Although I'm pensive.
I wish I could unwind,
And wallow in this pain—
It's so offensive.
She thinks I am less than a man,
And mocks me with every demand.

I'm challenged in my heart—
I know that I am more
Than what I'm feeling.
I've got to set apart
The essence of my core,
That you're revealing.
You tell me that I am still strong,
And fully a man all along.

I'm challenged in my soul—
I know my only source
Is God eternal.
He made life to be whole,
And understands of course,
When it's infernal,
And when I am challenged like this,
He lifts me up from the abyss.

He said that he was mentally challenged, left speechless while confronting the relentless demands and denigrating treatment of a friend who was no longer being friendly. I softly and empathetically said, simply, "It's ridiculous." He replied, ever gently, "It's offensive," as he valiantly withheld his annoyance and extended amazing grace.

cloud

Come, cloud, it's OK,
I don't mind the way
Your airiness covers the skies.
Between clouds and sun,
I normally shun
The shadow of your bold disguise.

But now it is hot,
And I feel I'm not
Against how you gently diffuse
The stifling heat,
And so, cloud, let's meet,
Your highness, above me, my muse.

You come and you go,
And blow to and fro—
It's poetry, how you were made—
While I stand on earth,
I've been here since birth,
And finally welcome your shade.

19 Jul 2019

I avidly savor the sunshine, avoiding cloudy shadows.
But on this summer day, the heat was so sweltering that
I welcomed this one single cloud, its shade a soft and
glorious covering.

less and more

With less and less,
There's more of me.
I'm penniless,
But full and free,
For deep within my core,
I know I need no more.

I do not know,
I cannot say,
How as I go,
I find a way
To see that less is much—
It is the golden touch.

I am alive—
I breathe the air,
And fully thrive,
With love to spare,
And love is what I give
More freely as I live.

Love is my gold,
My precious stone,
Not bought or sold,
For love alone
Is free, and it is mine
And yours—it is divine!

2 Sep 2019

My friend was plodding through some severe financial constraints, and yet I could see that his generous spirit persevered, shining with graciousness better than gold.

no turkey

There is no turkey roasting,
No wafting of scents,
No serenade smell,
No menu that I'm boasting—
It doesn't make sense,
When life isn't well,
To stage such a holiday meal—
I'll tell you how I really feel.

The happiness I'm faking
I cannot explain,
But I only know
That while their pies are baking,
I'm feasting on pain—
It's not sweet, and so
I really want nothing to eat—
My holiday meal is no treat.

But what is this you're serving?
A genuine smile,
A loving embrace.
I feel so undeserving,
And yet for a while
I sample a trace
Of what this whole day is meant for—
I'm grateful and hungry for more.

28 Nov 2019

Not everyone has a happy Thanksgiving, especially when life's circumstances encroach on a heart that has already confronted so much hurt. When I expressed concern and care, it seemed to alter the landscape, even if only in my small and simple way.

angels

There are things that I cannot explain,
Though my quill makes a claim to much
    more.
I hear rhythm and rhyme all around,
And then poetry makes it profound.
All that happens, the pleasure and pain,
Is it vaporous legend and lore,
Something some would imagine, a whim,
Or a lyric less lovely, more grim?

Are there angels, right here and right now?
Who am I, then, to figure that out?
Their appearance, to many, seems odd—
Do they truly come here, sent by God?
Yes, I choose to believe, that is how
I discover that I have no doubt,
And with reason and rhyme as I write,
I see more with my poetic sight.

Then I looked, then I sensed, then I saw
What another eyewitness had seen—
Yes, an angel was there, very real,
Supernatural, making me feel
That this story so horrible, raw,
Has a meaning, but what does it mean?
This mysterious angel disguise
Is a poem of love to my eyes.

1 Dec 2019

When Shannon Kerr asked me to ghostwrite her survival story, a true account that includes the appearance of angels, I knew that this was a serious task not to be taken lightly. Far be it from me to fail at accurately representing the activities of angels, God's heavenly messengers. The result, *Against All Odds: An Incredible Journey of Hope and Healing*, is a gripping story of life and love, all by God's hand.

sweden: the ericson quest

A cottage clad in red,
A lake of melted blues,
Each tree a forest green,
A moose disguised ahead,
Its antlers branchy hues,
The trolls as yet unseen.

Lush berries in the wild,
The foraged ones we ate,
The bleak and blissful roe,
Our energies beguiled
By skies that darken late
In summer, lazy, slow.

In Sweden to explore
The cemetery trail,
The Ericsons of old,
And digging more and more,
The journey did not fail,
Both beautiful and bold.

We saw more than a grave,
A tombstone in the ground,
A homestead and a name,
For all of Sweden gave

Us life, and there we found,
Discovered and became.

We each became aware
Of meatballs at their best
And lingonberry jam,
And all that Swedish fare,
The condimented quest,
With you, is who I am.

12 Dec 2019

In 2015, three generations of my family traveled to Sweden to explore our Ericson family roots, the first time that anyone had done this since our ancestors emigrated in the 19th century. We sought traces in cemeteries and other historic sites, an astounding experience of discovering not only the past but also who we are today.

immanuel

Immanuel, God is with us,
Is with us right here and right now,
Not just then.
But somehow I'm wondering just
Exactly the meaning and how,
Still again,
Yes, how can God be
With you and with me?

God with us seems more like without
The tidings of comfort and joy
From above.
I struggle to figure it out,
When hatred just seems to annoy
All that love,
This struggle I hate,
But you say, "Just wait."

"Just wait and just listen," you say.
"The carols and tidings are true—
God is here.
Immanuel, then and today,
God with us, with me and with you,
Do not fear.
Fear not what you feel,
God with us is real."

22 Dec 2019

"'The virgin will conceive and give birth to a son, and they will call him Immanuel' (which means 'God with us')."
Matthew 1:23

climate change

Icebergs melt,
Species sputter,
Carbon climbs in the air.
Have you felt,
Trembled, shuddered,
With this global despair?
The change is climactic, the temperature
    hot—
Can we keep sustaining this planet or not?

Dare I say
That this worry
Isn't my main concern?
I won't play
Judge or jury,
But I will take my turn
To speak of the climate that I really feel—
It's all cataclysmic and globally real.

Love is cold,
Frozen, chilling,
Worse than the warming trend.
Young and old
Are just killing
Love to a stagnant end.
And this is our moment to turn it around—
Let's be eco-friendly, let's let love abound.

31 Dec 2019

"At that time many will turn away from the faith and will betray and hate each other, and many false prophets will appear and deceive many people. Because of the increase of wickedness, the love of most will grow cold, but the one who stands firm to the end will be saved. And this gospel of the kingdom will be preached in the whole world as a testimony to all nations, and then the end will come."
Matthew 24:10-14

shipwrecked

I do not know,
I cannot tell
The reason that I go.
The wind is strong,
This stormy swell,
This gusty, surging throng
Compels me, and somehow I must
Go forward and steadily trust.

I feel so weak,
So shipwrecked, lost
At sea, and still I seek
To stay intact,
While battered, tossed,
As faith encounters fact:
This storm is so real, I could die,
But God knows the sea and the sky.

God says, "Don't quit,
You will survive
The tempest, all of it
Is in my plan—
You are alive—
Take courage, weary man.
I'll carry you safely to shore—
Just trust me, then trust me some more."

2 Feb 2020

Based on the account of the shipwreck in Acts chapter 27, poem one of two written as a complement to my father's teaching.

still sailing

An angel didn't tell me,
I didn't see a sign,
But I must persevere.
The sea is churning fiercely,
This tumult in my mind,
My ship will wreck, I fear.
But I can't abandon this now—
My ship must sail onward somehow.

God holds the oars and rudder,
All firmly in his hands,
Securely in his grip,
And though my ship may shudder,
I don't look at the sands
That swirl around this ship.
Instead I consider God's care,
And know I can sail anywhere.

4 Feb 2020

Based on the account of the shipwreck in Acts chapter 27, the second of two poems that I wrote to support my father's lesson plan.

refueling

Do I need gasoline,
The putrid, liquid gold
That fuels mobility?
Yes, maybe so.
I'm somewhere in between
My engine running cold,
And what's inside of me,
And I say, "No."

Yes, let me tell you first,
Though I'm ashamed to talk:
I have no car at all,
No, not one wheel,
And what I really thirst,
Inside me as I walk,
Is such it might appall,
But let's be real.

I feel so dry inside,
My body is like rust,
My motor wants to quit—
Where are the keys?
And much as I have tried—
And try my best, I must—
I can't get over it.
Please help me, please.

Please tune me up at last,
And fill me to the line,
The tire pressure right,
But not too much,
So I can feel so fast,
Zoom, zooming, humming fine,
My struggles out of sight—
All by your touch.

8 Mar 2020

A friend was facing the challenge of paying bills while also keeping his car engine running, even to the point that he had to walk. Sometimes what each of us really needs is not only an auto mechanic and gasoline, but also the expertise of the one magnificent God who moves us forward.

fog

It's nebulous,
That's all I see—
The clouds, the mist, the grey,
So vaporous—
How can it be
The start of a new day,
A day without the sun,
Just foggy, just begun?

The atmosphere
Seems not awake,
Except for birds that sing.
They make it clear
That I should make
The most of everything,
While fog that fills the skies
God's praises would disguise.

The vapor just
Borrows the air,
And soon will dissipate—
Till then I must
Never despair
That I cannot create,
While God makes all things still,
And praise him yet I will.

30 Mar 2020

The morning started with sunless fog, and with it could also have come a fear that God is as absent as the sun. But no, he is worthy of worship in all of the cloudy stillness.

teardrops

So, what is today,
Or what is it not?
I don't know what at all.
I blink, look away,
And then, dot-dot-dot,
The tears begin to fall,
Each droplet its own trail
Of gravity, so frail.

I silently cry
For you and for me,
For all this thirsty land.
We cannot deny
The drought that we see,
The solemn reprimand
On all our soulless dust—
What of "In God we trust?"

The tears are for you,
For us, it is time
To quench our godless thirst.
Each drop falls like dew
On drought-stricken grime,
And this is just the first—
Tomorrow's thirsty song
Will seek God all day long.

1 Apr 2020

One day flows into another during the coronavirus quarantine, and in the quiet, the tears flow from repentant hearts reaching out to God.

love up above

Are you ready for joy,
Or does it not appeal,
While joyless is more real?
What if I could deploy
A message in the sky—
What then, a blissful sigh?

A brave and soaring kite,
A white and puffy cloud,
That sings to you out loud?
What if the stars could write,
Up high, way up above,
And spell just one word: love?

"That is just fantasy,
The stars don't spell," you say,
"Don't tease my sad dismay.
What's happening to me
Is harder than you know,
So take your joy and go.

But wait, just tell me this,
So I can comprehend
The message you intend.
In all your joyful bliss,
One word I can't ignore—
It's love, so tell me more."

Yes, love and joy and hope—
God's love shines now on you—
He cares, and I do too,
And while you try to cope,
So overwhelmed these days,
His love can lift your gaze.

2 Apr 2020

Coronavirus is no joke, but there is joy in God's constant love.

not the end

I wonder, how does it feel,
To know that death is not the end,
But only the beginning?
Should my countenance reveal
A joy I cannot comprehend,
While I'm so far from winning?

On my face I feel defeat,
And in my heart a doomsday dread,
As all hope evaporates.
This pandemic is discreet,
And also bold, so many dead,
The sad tally escalates.

I can see no end in sight,
As all life circles to a close,
But I have a nagging thought—
I remember one dark night,
Well, there were many, I suppose,
When I found the hope I'd sought.

I just waited for the dawn,
Though desperate darkness felt so long,
And then finally: the sun.
Life is like this, on and on,
And while this doomsday seems so wrong,
There is more—it's just begun.

There is more, and it is life,
Life beyond this endless dying—
Daybreak, life beyond the grave—
Resurrection amid strife,
Joyful tears instead of crying—
Jesus lives, and he can save.

7 Apr 2020

The doomsday darkness of the pandemic is a passing
thought in light of the life of Jesus.

the psalmist

I'm sure there's a psalm I could read—
The Lord is my shepherd, I know,
And right now he makes me lie down.
I have all the pasture I need,
Just like the psalm said long ago,
But something is making me frown.

So, why are you downcast, my soul,
And why so disturbed within me,
Aren't goodness and mercy enough?
The psalmist then comes to console—
Trust God, he is good, taste and see,
A rock when the waters are rough.

Yes, let everything that has breath,
All fearfully, wonderfully made,
Join in the deliverance song.
God shepherds me from birth to death—
I'll trust him and not be afraid—
The psalmist was right, all along.

9 Apr 2020

Sometimes when the pandemic presses in on us, all we
really need is to be refreshed by a psalm.

the plague

The playing field is leveled,
The princes are disheveled,
The chambermaids have all been sent away.
The gala's cancellation
Has ruined all elation,
The gossipers don't quite know what to say.

What of the fancy dresses?
And no one even guesses—
What will they do with all of that good
    food?
No buoyant, happy dances,
Not taking any chances,
And no one really is now in the mood.

The plague! It has invaded!
We thought we had evaded
The pestilence, but it has hit us now.
Both rich and poor are stricken
And feel the terror thicken—
If only royalty could help somehow.

The people are united,
Or then again, divided,
As everyone takes refuge, all alone.
The kingdom is upended,
All merriment suspended,
And far away I hear a deathly moan.

But then I hear a clatter—
What is it? What's the matter?
A sound so loud I can't hear anything.
It's chariots with banners!
I muster my best manners—
If only I could really see the king!

A messenger is waving,
And with each gesture saving
The hopes of all the people of the land.
He cries out: "Hear ye, hear ye,
The plague is ending, only
Keep trusting," thus behold the king's
      command.

11 Apr 2020

When the plague sweeps through the land, everything
stops and suffers, eager for it to pass.

kiss of rain

What is the language of rain?
Is it a speech or a song,
Or a verbose narrative?
Is the rain mad or insane,
Each drop together a throng,
Taunting the life that I live?

I only wanted to play,
Out in the soft-spoken air,
Skipping between each sunbeam.
Pelting, the rain seems to say,
"Stop all your frolic right there,"
Teasing, or so it would seem.

And now it's raining some more—
Where in the world is the sun,
When the whole sky is a cloud?
Just as I wondered before,
When is this craziness done,
Splashing and gushing out loud?

But then, a drop on my face,
Just as I'm dashing inside,
Bigger than all of the rest,
A playful kiss, an embrace
I couldn't stop if I tried—
Maybe the rain does know best.

13 Apr 2020

The rain might be a nuisance, or maybe not, really.

word friends

I don't write a poem myself—
My word friends are here, happily,
Up there, perching on the bookshelf,
Or sitting nearby, next to me—
They giggle and wink,
And help me to think.

They tell all their stories in rhymes,
Like artists, but with adjectives,
Their rhythm is wacky sometimes,
But poetry always forgives,
With license to be
Poetic and free.

They know other languages too,
A happy assortment, each word,
Each letter its own point of view,
But something has happened, absurd—
I'm empty, bereft—
My word friends have left.

I barely breathe and I can't smell,
The fever has sizzled my taste,
My body aches, I don't feel well—
This poem will all be a waste—
My pulsating brain
Can't think with this pain.

But then, in my feverish state,
The words whisper softly, "Don't fret.
We didn't abandon you, wait,
We're right here, right now—better yet,
Just rest and be calm,
While we read a psalm."

15 Apr 2020

Words are like inspiring friends, cheering us on as we write, and comforting us when we lack ideas.

social distancing

It's not that I can't stand to be alone,
I've had my share of days here on my own,
I know how to survive
And keep myself intact.
It's true that I'm alive,
But that's an empty fact,
When every day is one more, far from
    you—
I'll wait this out, it's all that I can do.

The protocols are keeping us apart,
But I will always hold you in my heart,
For that's where you belong,
Right here inside of me.
Take courage and stay strong,
Until we're finally free
To roam and wander almost anywhere,
And soon embrace the love that took us
    there.

16 Apr 2020

Social distancing stirs up a longing to love in proximity,
which we will do as soon as the pandemic subsides.

stronger still

I know that you are hardy, so am I,
But what if that last hug was that—the
    last?
And now I wonder why
The future is the past,
And all tomorrows turned into today,
When I am here, and you are far away.

We knew that death would come, sometime,
    somehow,
But this is different, I don't understand
The way I feel right now,
When I can't touch your hand,
Because of this invisible disease
That touches us when no one even sees.

My words are postcards full of platitudes:
"I miss you, and I wish that you were here,"
But my whole attitude
Is simple and sincere,
And while this plague is threatening to kill,
Today our love is stronger, stronger still.

17 Apr 2020

As the pandemic protocols press in on us, we start to
wonder if the last time we touched someone we love was
really the last time.

symptoms

The plague has hit you hard,
Although you're breathing fine.
It caught you here off guard,
So stealthy and unkind,
And brought everything to a halt,
While what you feel isn't your fault.

The pressure on your chest,
The temperature that rose,
Are symptoms that attest
To what I would suppose,
Is truly a sign of the strain
Of COVID-19 on your brain.

Your mind is all worn out,
So is the bank account,
You worry and you doubt,
How will you now remount
A business essential to you,
With clients who need what you do?

Well, first I will say this,
"Don't feel that you're alone,
God hears and doesn't miss
The anguish of your groan,
And he will bring clients your way—
Until then, we simply must pray."

And, second, I will add,
Oh, dear, beloved man,
"Take courage and be glad,
Together, yes we can
Prove to the pandemic that we
Are stronger than uncertainty."

17 Apr 2020

The symptoms of the pandemic are real, and we must trust that God surely has a rescue plan.

aroma of god

I'll tell you what's contagious,
Whenever I inhale,
It has the strangest scent.
Its fragrance is outrageous—
My senses sputter, fail,
And yet I feel content—
It grasps me, familiar yet odd,
It is the aroma of God.

It catches me unready,
And takes my breath away,
Then fills my lungs with air.
My pulse becomes unsteady,
Until my heart can say,
"I know that God is there."
Not artsy, remote or abstract,
It's palpable, purely a fact.

Because of the pandemic,
The air is calm and still,
While hesitant and shy.
Unease becomes endemic,
And no deep breath can fill
The vacuum of a sigh,
When grasping for more oxygen—
This isn't the breathing of zen.

But I am breathing deeply
Of something else outside—
It's like another sense—
Its gentleness surrounds me,
It soothes my soul inside,
Its poignancy intense,
And as I exhale, I tell you:
God loves you, he's here with you too.

19 Apr 2020

With all this talk of contagion in the air, what we really need to catch is the refreshing aroma of God's constant care.

unmasked

I have a petty complaint,
And though proper poets don't whine,
I can't just pretend that I'm fine.
It's somewhat risky to taint
What you would consider as right,
But I'm putting voice to my plight.

In this pandemic distress,
I still resist one protocol—
It's strictly much worse than them all.
I don't say this to confess
That I have defied the decree,
I'm just speaking poetically.

It's the strange rule of the mask—
It covers up half of the face,
While leaving the lips with no trace.
"What is the problem?" you ask,
"It's there so the virus is not—
They claim it protects us a lot."

I let you talk for a while,
Of how every cough, every sneeze,
Could easily spread the disease,
But what I miss is a smile
That's hidden in all of the fuss,
As masks make just monsters of us.

Behind each mask, we've succumbed
To a grim societal change,
While losing a grinning exchange.
As a result, we're all numbed
To this sad façade-like disguise,
Where we can see only the eyes.

As I regret this, I think
Of starting a new etiquette,
So when you see this, don't forget,
That if I look at you and wink,
I'm not bold, flirtatious or coy,
I'm only unmasking my joy.

21 Apr 2020

Wearing all these masks, we have lost the ability to see and share a smile, so why not a wink as an alternative?

vaccine

What if I invented a vaccine,
And it guaranteed
That we would be freed
From living here somewhere in between
The picture of health
And shadowy stealth?
What would all that freedom really mean,
With no grave concern
Or ill to discern?
Would life be a dead and dull routine?

Would it be just like this poem now,
With rhymes that repeat,
So tidy and neat?
Would it be much worse than this somehow,
A powerful shot
That makes our faith rot?
That is something I would not allow.
The vaccine would make
Our trust in God fake—
I don't like that sound, I will avow.

This idea has put me to the test—
I'm not really sure
What is the best cure.
Now it seems I really have digressed
From finding a way
To help, so I pray,

"God help all the experts do their best,"
While I do my part
To write from my heart—
Could a poem cure more than the rest?

23 Apr 2020

Would a vaccine really be better than this, if it robs us of
one of the best parts of persevering in this pandemic:
putting our trust in God?

box of treasures

I have a box of treasures,
It's underneath my bed—
Oh, what have I just said?
I shouldn't say exactly where it's stored.
It's full of tiny pleasures,
Like some would keep pet rocks.
Inside my little box,
It's worth much more than I could dare
    afford.

I thought of it this morning,
As soon as I awoke,
The words that I once spoke,
When life was free and uncontained back
    then.
Those words are now adorning
The darkness and the dust,
And someday soon I must
Retrieve the words I cherish once again.

The adjectives are longing
To get outside and paint
With fluid unrestraint—
They languish, having nothing to describe.
The nouns all lack belonging,
And feel so out of place—
They want a maskless face

To show them worlds and cultures with
    good vibe.

The verbs I hid are ready,
Inside there, tucked away—
They really want to play,
But this pandemic doesn't want a game.
And so, they're waiting, steady,
Until they can once more
Get out and go explore,
Then write of wonders that are there to
    claim.

The words I keep are smitten
With what they all desire—
They mingle and aspire
To get outside the box and travel far.
And then, once they have written,
Back to the box they'll go—
I told you, so you know
Exactly where my treasures really are.

25 Apr 2020

There are words and worlds left unexplored during this
pandemic, but when it passes, we can again discover and
write.

solitude

Solitude makes holiness seem easy,
Like a cloudless sky when it is breezy,
Windswept motives, pure—
This is right, I'm sure—
Anyone would certainly agree,
There is no one here to question me.

Solitude turns peace into an idol—
All alone, I value being idle—
Even when I toil,
No one else can spoil
All the peacefulness inside my mind—
I can work and play as I'm inclined.

Solitude makes loving too convenient—
Loving from afar is far too lenient,
Hypothetical,
And heretical,
I must love in action when I do—
Let's see if my godliness is true.

Solitude can teach me to be godly,
But in crowds, God is there too, and oddly,
Neither one is wrong,
Both can make me strong,
When God is the keeper of my soul,
Breathing like the wind, then I am whole.

25 Apr 2020

Solitude can give us the illusion that we are saints, until we get out into the world and put our godliness to the test.

conspiracy theory

If there is conspiracy,
Let it be known—
Go publish the grim theory
That you condone—
You call the pandemic a plot,
So, should I agree, should I not?

In this pandemonium,
COVID-19,
Stand up at a podium,
There in between
The world politicians, with news
That media dare not refuse.

You say it's just fictitious,
All this alarm,
And also, most suspicious
That the worst harm
Is what this whole lockdown has done
To all of the freedom you've won.

I don't know what's false or true,
It's so bizarre,
But I'll only caution you:
Be sure you are
Still adding more truth to the tale,
Because every falsehood will fail.

God will have the final word
On this disease,
And amid the news we've heard,
Let's all just please
Be careful that we're not engrossed
So much we don't trust God the most.

27 Apr 2020

There are conspiracy theorists who claim that the coronavirus is an invention. I would like to know the truth in all of this, but most importantly I want to trust God.

clouds of the unknown

Can I float away, like that cloud?
Did I really say that out loud?
I ponder as I hover,
And, floating, I discover
That this existence really is a dream,
And more adventurous than it would seem.

How can empty skies fascinate?
Doesn't endless blue just sedate?
Not if you're contemplative,
Or, like the clouds, creative,
When every shifting shape becomes a muse,
And sculptures dissipate in milky blues.

Doesn't the unknown terrify?
How can it inspire, sky on sky?
I wonder what is up there—
This dream is not a nightmare,
When I'm awake and grounded as I gaze
At clouds that brush the surface of my
    days.

Poised elusively, undefined,
Clouds evade my grasp, and I find
That when they scatter, unpinned,
God's way is in the whirlwind,
And I'm beneath the dustings of his feet,
While begging every cloud to not retreat.

What's above the sky, I don't know,
I'm just watching clouds, softly slow,
And as I ponder, pining,
I see the silver lining,
The blissfulness this interlude inspires,
When God commands the clouds as he
    desires.

29 Apr 2020

"The Lord is slow to anger but great in power; the Lord will
not leave the guilty unpunished. His way is in the
whirlwind and the storm, and clouds are the dust of his
feet." Nahum 1:3

sicker

Maybe I am sicker still,
Maybe I am deathly ill,
Sicker than I know.
Diagnose what's ailing—
Is my goodness failing?
Since when? Long ago?

I was always in my prime,
Never did I lack the time
To do endless good.
Was I an impostor,
With a regal posture
All misunderstood?

I had no aim to deceive,
But my heart needs a reprieve—
I'm not well at all.
While the sick are healing,
I'm uneasy, feeling
This is my downfall.

Who am I that I was spared?
Now my heart is nagging, scared,
Deeply in my soul.
I wasn't infected,
But this has affected
My life as a whole.

God is keeping me alive,
And I want to fully thrive,
As the days pass by,
Giving God the glory
For my good-willed story,
Till the day I die.

1 May 2020

While this poem isn't an all-inclusive package expounding
on the entire meaning of life, it prompts apparently good
people who are surviving the pandemic to think about
God's purposes in their lives as individuals.

poetic fantasy

Enough of your poetic fantasy—
Your cadence is completely out of sync—
Enough, I said, enough.
The world isn't so dreamy, can't you see?
And no one really cares what you might
    think—
Go write prosaic stuff.

The language of the planet is its prose,
And no one builds a kingdom with a rhyme,
So don't be so naïve.
Your poetry is pretty, I suppose,
But who on earth would call this world
    sublime?
No, that I can't believe.

Besides, your stanzas wrap up far too soon,
As if to say, "That's it, that's all there is."
You oversimplify.
I'd rather listen to a wordless tune,
Where at the end there is no prodding quiz:
"What do you think and why?"

I really hate the questions that you ask—
You see the world as if you see my heart,
And ask me if it's true.
Your rhyme won't change the world, but is
    your task

To paint a stunning portrait with your art,
And prod my point of view?

Well, maybe after all I can't resist
The poems that you've crafted, line by
    line—
They rhyme with something more.
There, hidden in the rhythm that I missed,
Is subtle hope, a hope that isn't mine—
What's that there for?

3 May 2020

Poetry may seem superfluous, but maybe that is because
people do not want to stop and take it to heart.

the pace of the sun

This isn't the leisurely lull of my youth,
The days when the sun would suspend
Its pace, and each ray was a friend.
My pastimes were simple, unhurried,
    uncouth,
With only my daydreams at play,
While summer sun languished all day.

The urgent concern was: I want some ice
    cream,
And on a good day for the beach,
I'd playfully beg and beseech.
It was so idyllic, or so it would seem,
The girlish delight to outrun
My shadow, and skip in the sun.

Now I'm still happy and joyful and free,
Except that my freedom requires
More orderliness of desires.
The tasks stand in line, and they all beckon
    me,
They all seem to utter my name—
Pandemic or not, it's the same.

But in this pandemic, I want to reset
The buzzing of constant alarm—
Which tasks can I skip with no harm,
Or how can I make it, sunrise to sunset,

And still have the time to explore
The dreams that I dreamed long before?

I'm not lackadaisical, losing my zest—
I still have the glee of a child,
But not every day can be wild.
The sun in this lockdown still struts east to
    west,
Just like it did, it's not a race—
God help me to keep that same pace.

5 May 2020

When we were children, the days seemed long, and the sun crawled slowly in its path. As we age, our pace picks up, but maybe we need to pause, capturing the carefree spirit of youth.

it matters

This is when it matters,
This is when what matters really shows.
I won't impose
On the world that shatters
What I really wish that it would do.
I can't imbue
This whole world with kindness like I
    would,
Although I should.

Where is kindness hiding?
Where is kindness hiding on the ground?
It is profound.
I am only chiding,
Though I really do mean what I say,
Day after day.
Where is kindness when I am in need?
Listen, take heed.

Love is what I'm feeling.
Love is what I feel when you are here,
When you are near.
Without you, I'm reeling,
In a world beyond what I can face,
Then you embrace
All I am and all that I stand for,
And love me more.

6 May 2020

Being unemployed in the coronavirus crisis accentuates the needs of life. When someone comes alongside to assist, their love says so much.

essentials

What are the subtle essentials?
How to distinguish potentials
From what I need most?
So much is greatly appealing,
But is it only my feeling
Or only a boast?
Some surely need beans and rice,
And for me that would suffice.

What are the things now forbidden,
Delayed, discarded and hidden
Behind protocols?
Some things can't wait for tomorrow,
Adding more sorrow on sorrow
While neediness calls,
So we must all improvise,
As you have done, I surmise.

What have we now lost forever?
Did all these protocols sever
Humanity's core?
We were not made to be separate,
And when alone, we are desperate,
Aching for more,
More of the basic delight—
Sharing humanity's plight.

What are we purely forgetting?
How are the protocols vetting
Our needs and desires?
Nothing essential has vanished,
None of the protocols banished
What living requires,
And at the top of the list,
Loving will not be dismissed.

7 May 2020

The pandemic protocols put things into categories:
essential and non-essential. But what they cannot prohibit
is love.

carefree

I don't hear the silent panic anymore.
I think I've caught my breath now from the
    scare—
Should I care?
Life will never be the same as long before.
I hardly miss the things that I once had—
Is that bad?

It could never be much better than these
    days—
I'm free to roam, at least within my mind,
As designed.
There is always something more to dream—
    always.
Again tomorrow I will contemplate—
I can't wait.

All the days meander, carefree—so do I,
Oblivious to all the panicked noise—
I have poise.
I'm not unaware—I watch it with one eye,
And see the virus far away from me,
While I'm free.

But I know this can't go on and on and on,
And hope when long deferred makes the
    heart sick—
I must pick,

So I choose to think that when these days
    are gone,
God will hold my hopes and dreams, hold
    me too,
All anew.

9 May 2020

The carefree interlude of dreamy days cannot last forever, and God will carry me and my dreams forward as he wishes.

happy flower

This is makeshift happiness,
This is good enough, I guess—
Good enough for me.
Good is not the same as great,
But I'd rather live than wait,
While, expectantly,
I still hope for great and greater—
May it come sooner than later.

I expected more than this,
And I redefined my bliss,
Glad to be alive.
Happy is as happy does,
And I'm happy now because
I'm still here to thrive.
Life is like a fleeting flower
That the wind will soon devour.

I'm here, agile in the breeze,
And my happy heart agrees,
I can sway and dance,
When the winds of change are strong,
And the suffering is long—
This is now my chance
To display a joy unending,
While my fragile stem is bending.

Other fields of flowers die—
Will the tempest pass me by?
I don't know for sure.
If I wither, worrying,
I'd be only hurrying
What might not occur,
So, with nimble petals ready,
I choose happiness already.

11 May 2020

Perseverance in the pandemic requires agility, the ability to
remain happy, regardless.

that day in capernaum

Let's talk about Jesus today—
No really, please don't go away,
I just have a story to tell.
I see you so scared of disease,
So listen, just please listen, please—
I won't simply say, "All is well."

I know it all seems so remote—
The miracles, the fishing boat—
But it isn't legend or lore.
I lived by that famed Galilee,
Where he navigated the sea
And walked as if firm on the shore.

You've probably heard now and then
Of Peter and John and the men
Who followed him closely behind,
In Galilee and far beyond,
Where Jesus would teach and respond
To hearts while he read every mind.

Capernaum was my hometown,
Where Jesus came and settled down,
Though I didn't see him sit much.
My daughter was Peter's good wife,
And Jesus [gasp] once saved my life—
I'm breathing because of his touch.

I lay with a fever in bed
And couldn't get up, so instead
They brought Jesus close to my side.
He looked at me, holding my hand,
Then helped me up so I could stand—
I stood amazed—I'd almost died.

The rest of the day is a blur,
But not because of the fever—
I just was so eager to serve.
I asked Jesus what he would wish.
He wanted to eat some fresh fish,
So then I cooked without reserve.

The sickness I almost forgot,
But I still remember a lot
The gentle, compassionate care,
When Jesus held my hand in his—
I'm telling you just as it is,
And Jesus can go anywhere.

13 May 2020

"As soon as they left the synagogue, they went with
James and John to the home of Simon and Andrew.
Simon's mother-in-law was in bed with a fever, and they
immediately told Jesus about her. So he went to her, took
her hand and helped her up. The fever left her and she
began to wait on them." Mark 1:29-31

I have seen the house of Peter's mother-in-law in
Capernaum, where this captivating story happened. The
power and loving care of Jesus, in healing this precious
woman, still strike me today.

living with fear

They say we have to learn to live with
    fear—
That's what the experts are saying—
That's what they say, but what I really
    hear,
It hurts my ear,
Is all the trust they're betraying.

We trust them with what's good and just
    and right—
I like to think that they're trying—
They say that now there is no end in sight
For this bad blight—
I sure don't think that they're lying.

It's all uncertain, I do understand,
The cure is as yet elusive.
The virus is so strong, it's out of hand—
No reprimand
Will kill it and be conducive.

But back to something I had mentioned
    first,
All of the fear that just hovers.
In all of this, that is perhaps the worst,
As if we're cursed—
From the fear no one recovers.

In fearfulness and fright, where is the
    trust,
Where has God gone in the worry?
Don't neglect precautions, and yet we must
Quickly adjust
And trust God in a hurry.

15 May 2020

This week an authority said that we have to learn to live
with fear. I think we need an alternative.

the gallery

Such pointillism in the evergreens,
As if it were a gallery of art—
A curator might tell me what it means,
As every speckled brushstroke plays a part.

Each branch is dipped in fondant, candy-
    sweet,
A chartreuse color—does it taste of mint?
The deeper background shade is more
    discreet,
Like emeralds without sparkle, without
    glint.

And now my glance goes upward to the
    skies,
Where mottled blues and greys and creams
    combine—
A soft impressionism to my eyes,
As cotton, silk and linen intertwine.

The wildflowers seem to say, "Let's play,"
Some more exuberant and others shy—
Their palette is a vivid, bright array
The artist didn't want to simplify.

The stillness is suspended by a bird
That flutters past a flower next to me—

It's not alone because another stirred
And soared toward the horizon breezily.

I want to linger longer just to stare
At beauty that the painter will reveal—
The ferns are lacy marvels over there,
So fresh and delicate, like how I feel.

The sun now crafts more shadows in the
    trees,
Where wrinkled leather trunks stand
    sturdy, tall—
Magnificent, it brings me to my knees,
Since I know God, the artist of it all.

17 May 2020

The artistry of creation is astoundingly beautiful, and even
better when we know the Creator.

enough hope

If you have enough hope, never mind.
If you never despair,
You are better than most,
But I question it: Are you resigned,
Or perhaps unaware
And completely engrossed?

Do you practice your strong and brave
    face?
Is it mostly a smile,
Or a neutral façade?
Your strange posture seems so out of
    place—
It just isn't your style,
Makes your countenance odd.

Take a look and see what you've become,
Trying hard to be strong,
When you're trembling inside.
As the days go by, you feel more numb,
Since you've known all along
All those feelings you hide.

Oh, I really am sorry to pry,
With my bold empathy
And this long questionnaire.
I can see that you're starting to cry—

I'll pretend I don't see,
And just show you I care,

By disclosing what I also feel:
Yes, I'm sometimes afraid,
Overwhelmed by it all,
But then that's when my hope is most real,
Since God always has made
Himself big when I'm small.

I have just one more question for you,
So please ponder this one
And then answer it right:
Do you have the same hope that I do?
If your hope is undone,
I'll share mine with delight.

19 May 2020

People may claim that they have hope, but if we probe
further, we may find that, internally, they are crying out for
God, for a hope that will not fail.

now and not yet

Not yet is more powerful than now,
And now we are living in not yet,
But we must not forget
The gentle power as we wonder how
Life will ensue.

If we never felt expectancy,
But only the action of the day,
Our hope would go away,
And we'd be caught in our consistency,
Which sure won't do.

As if we all fear that the surprise
Won't be what our longings most desire,
And yet we must aspire,
While knowing God is good and strong and
    wise
In all that's new.

If we let not yet be in God's hands,
And if we relinquish our control,
Our hope will be more whole,
While trusting that God fully understands
Our point of view.

And so, while we wait, we more than cope,
Because of the powerful suspense,

Until God will commence
To merge the now and not yet with our
    hope—
May it be true.

21 May 2020

Hope has a swelling, surging power when we put our trust
in the sovereign God, now and through all of the not yet.

cravings

Think about your cravings and discern,
What is now forbidden, that you crave?
What is now on hold, of your desires?
Maybe in your thinking you will learn
How the protocols make you behave,
What this whole pandemic still requires.

This is just to get you thinking more—
We all need to think a little bit,
To determine who we really are.
Settle down your thoughts and go explore—
If a crazy thought comes, question it.
In your thinking, wander near and far.

What are all the things that you most miss,
Since you're not allowed to go and touch?
Don't let all this thinking go to waste.
When the rules are loosened after this,
Will you just say, "Thank you very much,"
And then go on with your hurried haste?

Or will you go see a land unseen,
Letting fresh priorities align,
Maximizing every latent trait?
Let God lead you now and in between—
He will be the best one to combine
Every part of you that is innate.

Here, I'll add one subject to your thought:
God is love, and he created you—
Filter that thought into all your dreams,
And you'll realize that you really ought
To let him define your cravings too—
Then life will be better than it seems.

23 May 2020

As we dream about what we wish we could do, we do best
to allow God to determine our big dreams.

the scandal of the mouth

The scandal of the mouth is scandalous.
The silent smugness is ridiculous.
No nasty words come out—
That's good, but what about
The speechlessness that is calamitous?

What is it that I know, that I resist?
Of what does faith in God, in fact, consist?
I claim that I believe,
But then I still deceive,
By thinking that I fail if I insist.

The person on the street may want to hear
About the hope I have—what do I fear?
No really, tell me why—
What is it—am I shy,
Or worried that my language won't be
    clear?

Or maybe I don't want to push and shove,
As if my firm belief puts me above
The person on the street,
Who really wants to meet
And know more of this Jesus, my first love.

Perhaps that is just it—my love is weak,
And if that is the case, my faith is bleak.
I want my life to be
More Jesus, less of me,
And full of love in everything I speak.

Oh, open up my mouth, Jesus, I pray,
And season every word that I will say,
With salt and love and light,
That by your grace I might
Tell someone else about you still today.

25 May 2020

"Let your conversation be always full of grace, seasoned with salt, so that you may know how to answer everyone." Colossians 4:6

"But in your hearts revere Christ as Lord. Always be prepared to give an answer to everyone who asks you to give the reason for the hope that you have." 1 Peter 3:15

not late

Am I ready yet?
I almost forget
What that is supposed to mean.
I'm not often late,
And yet as I wait,
I'm caught somewhere in between.

The virus is bad,
Far worse than I had
Awareness there at the start.
It shocked me, for sure,
And since there's no cure,
I took the lockdown to heart.

It drags on and on,
Old habits are gone,
And now I have a new pace,
Creative and free
To simply be me—
No schedule, only a trace.

The watch I don't wear
Is still ticking there—
Surely I will be on time,
For what is today,
And I dare to say
I'm feeling fine, in my prime.

But when this has passed,
I won't be the last
To be present as I must.
Don't call me late, no—
I'll show up and show
The love of the God I trust.

27 May 2020

Previous habits and schedules have slipped away in the pandemic, and still I am prepared to show up and not be late to love.

the pulse

This never static life is hardly slow—
The steady pulsing started long ago—
If you don't hear the beat,
Then listen with your feet,
And feel the rhythm coming from below.

The other pulse I hear is in the sky,
The flapping of the wings as the birds fly—
The clouds are their terrain,
And, singing, they sustain
The shrill pulsation that my ears decry.

The insects that I see don't make a sound,
Although they pulse and scamper all
    around,
To nibble on a leaf
Or find some short relief
From all their leggy flurry on the ground.

Or maybe what I hear is in my head—
Dynamic drumbeat, thinking far ahead.
With nothing else to blame,
I settle down my claim,
Admitting that the pulse is mine instead.

It's good to know my heart is beating,
    strong,

With energy that pulses all day long,
And yet, may I have poise,
While softening the noise,
And let God tap the tempo of my song.

29 May 2020

The dynamic pulsation persists, even in the pandemic lockdown, and we need to let God determine everything.

in the streets

Today we're inundated by this grief—
No smile and no mask,
Because we sadly ask:
When will we ever find some true relief?

The streets were empty only yesterday,
No quorum anywhere,
The intersections bare,
As we all struggled to keep death at bay.

But now, pandemic pandemonium—
This is no lockdown phase—
The streets are all ablaze,
As bullets hit us with what we've become.

It's black and white and more than that at
    stake,
It's anger and contempt,
As wounded hearts attempt
To see what kind of statement they can
    make.

Before, we touted such togetherness,
A common enemy,
A virus none can see,
But now we've added color to distress.

As if we hadn't counted every grave,
We're multiplying hate,
To only aggravate
The grim statistics no one can outbrave.

The violence, revenge and civil war
Are not a new disease—
Oh, God, just help us, please,
And heal this land that needs you more and
    more.

31 May 2020

Today we are struck by the sobering reality of racism, with rioting in the streets adding to the pervasive sadness of the pandemic.

ada maranda

Ada Maranda, baby, oh, baby,
I wonder if maybe,
Maybe your life was cut short.
Eight little months, I wish it were longer,
Wish you were stronger—
What is a death of this sort?

I never knew you—I would have liked to,
But then you never grew,
With not even time to talk.
Starting and ending, all in a heartbeat—
Tiny hands, tiny feet,
That never once learned to walk.

Those last 19 days that ended in tears,
Were followed by years
Of wondering how to feel.
Although it is sad, God made no mistake,
And your life was not fake—
Baby, your life was so real.

Ada Maranda, followed by many,
I don't know of any
Words that would really console.
Since 1860, we're still lamenting
More death and inventing
Ways to make life feel more whole.

God sees each as precious, loved to the last,
In this present and past,
More than a tombstone can tell.
Ada Maranda, I tell others now
Of God's great love and how
Life and death aren't just farewell.

2 Jun 2020

"Ada Maranda, daughter of Benjamin & Anna Buch, died April 5, 1860, aged 8 months & 19 days." I came across these words on a tiny tombstone in a small plot on the side of the road and paused to imagine the heartbreak of her parents.

i don't know the day

I don't know the day,
I don't know the hour,
Nor have I the power
To soothe and allay
The itch that you're feeling
For deep-tissue healing.

The subtle malaise
Squats under the surface,
Subverting your purpose.
You lurk in a daze,
An utter existence
Of grit and persistence.

It's no party game,
No longer amusing,
Although you're refusing
To temper and tame
The angst and the anguish,
Preferring to languish.

What good does it do
To trust what you can't see,
To wait and be antsy?
When will God renew
This world he created,
That seems so ill-fated?

I know what you mean—
The wait feels unending,
But I'm not pretending,
And though it's unseen,
The healing has started,
So don't be downhearted.

Please do this instead:
Be watching, be ready,
And keep your hope steady,
Because Jesus said
That he is returning
With joy for the yearning.

4 Jun 2020

"Therefore keep watch, because you do not know the day
or the hour." Matthew 25:13

in spite of his wonders

In spite of his wonders,
They did not believe,
Considered as blunders
To briefly bereave—
To him it was sin,
Observed with chagrin.

Futility followed,
With terror behind,
And as their hearts wallowed,
Corrupt, misaligned,
They soon had enough,
When trials got tough.

Then, done compromising
Their feeble belief,
They'd turn, recognizing
A need for relief,
Remembering, then,
To seek him again.

Their lips would just flatter,
Their tongues were a lie,
With meaningless chatter,
As faith became sly,
The oath of each heart,
Then falling apart.

Yet God, in his mercy,
Chose not to destroy
Their stiff controversy,
And didn't deploy
The fullness of wrath,
The grim aftermath.

He chose to remember
That they were but flesh,
And didn't dismember,
But came to refresh
A mere passing breeze,
Such people as these.

Abhorrent and shocking,
This stern history,
And yet I'm not mocking,
Because woe is me
If I am not sure
That my heart is pure.

And who of us ever
Is better, in fact,
When God has forever
Been what we most lacked,
And still is today
Our God, come what may.

6 Jun 2020

"In spite of all this, they kept on sinning; in spite of his
wonders, they did not believe. So he ended their days in

futility and their years in terror. Whenever God slew them, they would seek him; they eagerly turned to him again. They remembered that God was their Rock, that God Most High was their Redeemer. But then they would flatter him with their mouths, lying to him with their tongues; their hearts were not loyal to him, they were not faithful to his covenant. Yet he was merciful; he forgave their iniquities and did not destroy them. Time after time he restrained his anger and did not stir up his full wrath. He remembered that they were but flesh, a passing breeze that does not return." Psalm 78:32-39

the poet's voice

Today I took a break
And didn't write a thing,
Not wanting to sound fake
And pitifully cling
To some poetic rhyme,
As speechless as a mime.

The break was meant to be
A mindless interlude,
Unhindered and carefree,
But it was misconstrued
When my unyielding brain
Then started to complain.

Was it not yesterday,
Beneath a boundless sky,
That I'd said, "Seize the day?"
So why then, tell my why,
Would I not wield a pen
And write some more again?

My heart agreed, of course—
My brain was surely right—
And so with some remorse,
I came again to write
And seize the day before
It's gone forevermore.

The break was worth it, though—
So short and yet so sweet,
Confirming what I know,
That I don't dare retreat,
Because I have no choice—
I have a poet's voice.

So here I am, with joy,
The poet and her muse,
To prod but not annoy,
Because I can't refuse
To stir the world at best
With all that I've expressed.

8 Jun 2020

As a poet, I can pause for refreshment, but I cannot resist
speaking. My place in this world is to not be silent.

idyllic

Idyllic? No, no, not at all,
Unless there is something that I don't
    recall.
A furtive glance or a full stare
Will cause you to question your painterly
    flair.

Just hold your brush and look around,
And see all the movement that aches to
    resound—
It's not ideal, so don't suppose
That this is a still life in mild, demure pose.

The birds often squabble and fight,
Bombarding intruders with gall in plain
    sight.
The vultures are shrewd when they're still,
First spying, then swooping to seize a fresh
    kill.

And even the small birds are bold—
The early one catches the worm, so I'm
    told.
We don't even know what they sing—
Perhaps they are scolding a naughty
    nestling.

The skies are no sweet fairy tale,
But don't be disheartened, your painting
   won't fail,
As long as you're not so naïve,
With brushstrokes so gentle, you nearly
   deceive.

And now I recall one thing more,
Not sure how you'll paint it, but that is
   your chore,
Selecting the palette and tone—
It's almost idyllic, so paint, make it known.

God cares for each bird in the sky,
And none can outfly him, escaping his eye,
His eye and his kind, loving hand,
That holds every creature all over the land.

10 Jun 2020

The landscape may look idyllic, but the activities of the
birds are not always pretty. The same with our incessant
lives, pandemic or not, where the true beauty is being in
God's hands.

no record of wrongs

See that cloud, a speck in the sky?
That is where your heartache belongs,
Misty, vanishing, like a sigh,
For love keeps no record of wrongs.

Not to say your tears have no worth,
But they'll dissipate from your mind,
When God makes new heavens and earth,
And your worries swiftly unwind.

All the wrongs are now in the past,
Since love is no sour, bitter scribe,
And no tear can ever outlast
The new heavens none can describe.

Former wrongs and worries, once proud,
Can't subsist with love in the air—
They'll disperse, be gone like a cloud,
Cleansing every cry, everywhere.

That is what is coming ahead,
In the world that God will create—
You can sulk right now or, instead,
Love already—I wouldn't wait.

12 Jun 2020

"Love . . . keeps no record of wrongs." 1 Corinthians 13:4-5

"See, I will create new heavens and a new earth. The former things will not be remembered, nor will they come to mind." Isaiah 65:17

in the atmosphere

A cloudy sky can't be a faithful friend—
Like tumbleweed, it fumbles in a breeze,
Like choppy waves upon the open seas,
The clouds will blow into a formless end.

A cloudless vault is still no better chum,
A vast expanse of nothingness in vain,
Avoiding any promises of rain,
A bland and friendless sapphire, strangely
    glum.

The sun is overbearing when it shines,
Or so it seems to some in summer's heat,
When piercing rays don't offer a retreat,
And blatant beams extend no good lifelines.

But worse than that are shadows in the
    dark,
The nights that hide each effervescent star,
When friendly constellations hang afar,
And vivid blackness hovers, blinding, stark.

The skies can comfort with placidity,
And silently embrace the earthly sphere,
But love is never in the atmosphere,
Apart from God, who made it, you and me.

14 Jun 2020

Love is in the air only because God is love.

the whisper

If this is a whisper, then what is a shout?
I don't think I ever will figure that out,
Since I can't stand up to this sound—
It's deafening, makes my heart pound.

If this is the fringe, then how grand is the
cloak?
Each filament hangs on the words he just
spoke,
While bidding my longings depart,
And weaving a way to my heart.

If this is the thunder, then where should I
hide,
While cowering, trembling, confessing my
pride?
Such power I can't comprehend,
Since even the lightning bolts bend.

And as my heart cringes, a part of me
aches
To trust him for refuge when everything
quakes,
As if in my fear my soul knows
That love goes wherever God goes.

16 Jun 2020

"And these are but the outer fringe of his works; how faint the whisper we hear of him! Who then can understand the thunder of his power?" Job 26:14

world awareness day

This is an awareness day,
I hope that you're aware,
Not to fight a cause, per se—
So much of that to spare—
Some fight for more, some fight for less,
A constant quest for happiness.

Here we make a point to voice
What matters most to us—
More a duty than a choice,
To speak of thus and thus,
We verbalize what matters most,
We raise a glass, we raise a toast.

Each one has a different view
Of happiness for all—
Some are noble, good and true,
Some lack the wherewithal
To make the world a better place,
To temper renegade disgrace.

Some just end in tit for tat
And hardly change a thing—
This is so much more than that,
So let's be focusing
And be aware, look left and right—
Where is there pain? Where is there plight?

This is world awareness now,
And let us not suppose
We can sit around somehow,
While all the NGOs
Will keep their eyes on everyone,
For at that rate, it won't get done.

Now is when you must arise,
Be present where you are,
Listen for the silent cries
And catch a falling star,
And if you speak, then let it be
A word of love, said happily.

18 Jun 2020

There seems to be a day for every cause imaginable on this earth, and yet what we need to do as individuals is care deeply for those in our area of influence.

fascination

Always one step ahead
And almost outpacing the wind,
Swirling high overhead,
So innocent, undisciplined,
Their borders are shadows of grey,
With freedom to wander away.

Teasing with their charade,
Each glimpse is a chapter they tell,
Characters all arrayed,
A mottled collage as they spell,
With page after page after page,
A promenade across a stage.

Sometimes they all conspire,
Creating a sinuous plot,
Climbing higher and higher,
And ask if I'm watching or not,
While knowing my answer is clear,
Since I'm always watching from here.

Every instinct in me
Looks upward to gape and to gaze,
Far beyond gravity,
Where weightlessness tents all my days
And shifting shapes pose for my eyes,
Unwittingly to mesmerize.

I will scarcely admit
That sometimes their bliss is replaced
When they darken and spit,
Their passive play quickly erased,
But even while tumbling, they tease,
And coax me to watch them at ease.

There is something like awe
That grips me in my upward glance—
I can barely withdraw
From keeping my pondering stance.
So why do the clouds fascinate?
I think it is God more than fate.

20 Jun 2020

My fascination with clouds comes not from fate but from
God.

frugality

What has frugality earned you so far,
What has it done to your debt?
How has your hoarding now changed who
    you are,
How has it made you forget
That all of the pocketed kindness is not
Of worth any longer, because it will rot?

What is this frugal mentality for,
Making you leery to spend?
Don't you remember what God did before,
Or do you only pretend
To trust that God feeds you like each little
    bird?
For when you cry, hungry, he already
    heard.

You just live once, so you better think twice
About frugality's cost.
I didn't venture to give you advice,
Until I saw you were lost—
You're lost in a fear that you only invent
And calculate every last cent that you
    spent.

See how you're cheating yourself from the
    best—
Don't you know quality counts?

But what is worse is how you treat the rest
With all your frugal discounts—
You're building up debt that you ought to
    repay—
Go spend yourself, loving, and never delay.

22 Jun 2020

Be leery of being frugal to a fault, and be sure to love freely.

repentance and rest

In repentance and rest,
In rest and repentance,
You would find the salvation you seek.
But I never had guessed,
That your independence,
Would imprison you now as I speak.

In quietness and trust,
In trust and in quiet,
There was strength, but you did not come
    close.
Instead you simply thrust
Your heart toward a riot,
Where your clamor is your only boast.

You would flee on a horse,
Instead of believing
In the rescue that God will soon send.
Don't you feel some remorse
For fleeing and grieving
The great God on whom you can depend?

God longs to be gracious,
To show you compassion,
To bring justice into your despair,
So don't be audacious
And flee in your passion—
If you trust God, he will be right there.

24 Jun 2020

"This is what the Sovereign Lord, the Holy One of Israel, says: 'In repentance and rest is your salvation, in quietness and trust is your strength, but you would have none of it.' Yet the Lord longs to be gracious to you; therefore he will rise up to show you compassion. For the Lord is a God of justice. Blessed are all who wait for him!" Isaiah 30:15, 18

as in a mirror

The image, the figure, the shadow is dim,
In seeing, I barely can see.
I see just the hint of an outline, a rim,
Of what I know knowledge to be,
And nothing is clear,
The more that I peer.

It's like an enigma I polish and clean,
And sometimes the surface is scratched,
And then, too, I wonder, what does it all
    mean,
And why are my questions unmatched
By answers that show
What I want to know?

The more that I'm gazing, I hardly see
    much—
It's like a reflection, a glint,
Yet something still grips me, a gentle,
    strong clutch,
Invisible now as I squint,
Convincing my mind
That I am not blind.

The love of God captures my soul, and my
    eyes
See all through this filter for now,
And loving God is what I know to be wise,

While later, someday and somehow,
Much more than a trace,
I'll see face to face.

26 Jun 2020

"For now we see only a reflection as in a mirror; then we shall see face to face. Now I know in part; then I shall know fully, even as I am fully known." 1 Corinthians 13:12

"Whoever loves God is known by God." 1 Corinthians 8:3

the calmness you crave

Go rest your weary head
That seems to pound there on its own.
Your heart can't get ahead,
With your head beating all alone—
The calmness you crave is elusive,
And all your attempts inconclusive.

You strive and strive and strive,
As if your gain were up to you,
And plans that you contrive
Just fall apart the more you do—
Are all of the goals you're pursuing
A painful, disgraceful undoing?

This ailment no one knows
Is a pandemic side effect—
You're aching for repose,
And there's a symptom I detect—
I see you're alone, agonizing—
Don't worry, I'm not criticizing.

I feel for what you feel,
The pounding and the ache,
The pain that you conceal,
So let us not forsake

The refuge of peace in the pounding,
Where God's peace is greatly resounding.

28 Jun 2020

"Let them come to me for refuge; let them make peace
with me, yes, let them make peace with me." Isaiah 27:5

a picture

I almost took a picture of a flower—
It was orange, it was yellow, it was green—
But then I paused, not wanting to devour
That brief moment with an image on a
    screen.

I somewhat felt a selfishness of spirit,
As I struggled—should I share or should I
    not?
But as I crept up closer there, right near it,
To my spirit came another afterthought.

Who said that I am selfish for observing
A small flower on a sunny afternoon,
As if, when I'm alone I'm undeserving
Of sheer happiness, unless I share it soon?

For, surely, my ideal is to be sharing,
But sometimes I need to stop and simply be,
While gathering fresh memories, not
    sparing
The best details to then tell you what I see.

But be assured, I'll take another photo,
Because beauty always begs me to persist,
To capture in an instant here, just solo,
And then share with you the picture of my
    bliss.

30 Jun 2020

In moments of beauty, we must find the balance between being present and passing along our bliss.

in the background

There are others in the background, just as
    pretty,
Invisible and hidden there, unseen,
And then now I start to wonder, almost pity,
What their feelings are, stuck there in
    between.

There they are, between the beauty and the
    background,
By no fault of theirs, planted far behind—
They can dream, but they forever will be
    earthbound,
And what is pretty when it is confined?

There are blossoms that don't always get
    the limelight—
Although beautiful, no one seems to see,
And the shadows often find them in the
    sunlight,
While their petals bud and bloom perkily.

There is mystery in who gets the attention,
When a pretty flower stands here obscure,
And today I'll look more closely, with
    intention,
At the brave and beautiful and demure.

There is something fascinating and amazing
In the way God sees it all, every one,
And today as I am focusing and gazing,
God's awareness can never be outdone.

2 Jul 2020

I took a picture of a beautiful purple flower that had
grabbed my attention in just one glance. When I passed
by it again later, I noticed the other beauties in the
background.

hopeful misfit

If you're counting up the hopeful, count me
   in,
Though it seems that you're not ready to
   begin,
While you tally up the miseries and woes,
Which is good enough for you, so you
   suppose.

Is there something satisfying in your mind
When you see how everything is misaligned,
Since the company of misery is sweet,
And you feel assured, the more woes that
   you meet?

To the litany of sorrow and lament,
You can add your own applause and your
   assent,
Because everybody likes to think out loud,
And all misery is better in a crowd.

But then aren't you ever curious at all
To discover something better and recall
That despite your odd contentment just to
   mope,
I had said that you could count on me for
   hope?

I admit that this whole planet isn't well,
But I'm still a hopeful misfit, can't you tell?
Because while this world is one gigantic
    mess,
I know God is doing more than we can
    guess.

4 Jul 2020

Better than complaining along with the crowd is choosing
to hold onto hope in God.

a melody not a malady

I have a melody, not a malady,
Though it may seem that I'm ill,
And there is nothing here of insanity,
Even if it might sound shrill.

So please don't try to claim that I've lost
    my mind,
While I sing my happy song,
Because it's not my fault if you trail behind
And don't want to sing along.

It may seem strange to sing while the world
    is sick,
And a song is not a cure,
But since the choice is mine, I just choose to
    pick
What will help me to endure.

What is this joy, joy, joy in the pain, pain,
    pain
That surrounds me all around?
Why do I sing as if it is not in vain,
While I hear no happy sound?

So let me say one word, though it might
    offend,

"It is Jesus, he's the one
Who gives me joy beyond what I
        comprehend,
And the song has just begun."

6 Jul 2020

The line "a melody, not a malady," from "Cloud Atlas,"
captivated me because I have a song that may seem crazy.

holding my passport

What is a passport, if I cannot pass
Through the unyielding, tall fence?
I watch with longing through walls made of
    glass,
And it all gleams with suspense.

There is a boundary, a solid line,
That I cannot jump across,
And if I claim that this passport is mine,
No one attends to my loss.

Having a passport does not make me free
To travel just on a whim—
I am a fish that cannot find the sea,
Captured, unable to swim.

On the horizon, the glassy, strong wall
Postures to keep me in place—
I am restricted, at no fault at all,
Due to this viral disgrace.

Someday I'll travel, or then maybe not—
When will the fence have a door?
I'll hold my passport, and I'll hold this
    thought,
Ready to go, like before.

8 Jul 2020

With the pandemic restrictions prohibiting me from traveling to Portugal, I hold my passport, watching and waiting.

pretty all around

Do you have an ugly side,
Or are you pretty all around?
Is there anything you hide,
Maybe more dingy, less profound?

I see petals I admire—
Each one is orange, bursting, bright—
Underneath them, is there mire,
Or perfect beauty, good and right?

Passing by a flower now,
I see its beauty, bending low—
Imitating it, I bow—
And, stooping closer, now I know.

Underneath the grand display,
There is more beauty, out of view—
Like these petals, can you say
That you are pretty, through and through?

10 Jul 2020

I passed by a bright orange flower that was beautiful when
viewed from above and also from below, and I pondered—
is my heart purely pretty from all angles?

107

One hundred seven or one hundred eight,
More than a lifetime of years—
If I live that long, will I be sedate,
Or will I lead all the cheers?

Death takes some early, but not everyone—
Others live longer than most,
And if my journey has only begun,
I have no valiant boast.

I only know that this life is not mine,
Nothing to claim as my own—
Maybe a century is my design,
And I will not be alone.

With God, the future is more than the past,
Ample, decreasingly poor—
And so, I want all my dreams to outlast
One hundred seven and more.

12 Jul 2020

I received the news that a relative, Eva Sundin, had died
in Sweden on Friday at the age of 107, not due to the
pandemic, after a long and wonderful life. And I realized
that I was not prepared to live that long.

out of sync

So, what do you think,
Is life out of sync,
While promises sing out of tune?
The song has become
A half-life, dull, numb,
And soon means much later than soon.

When is there an end
We can comprehend,
Since we are restricted by time?
It all seems so late,
And we cannot wait
To add to a word one more rhyme.

If we would but trust,
We would readjust
Our sick misperception of loss.
We toss and we turn
And struggle to learn
The point of each turn and each toss.

With so much at stake,
Let's make no mistake
And think that God left us for dead,
When what we should do,
Between me and you,
Is live in God's love as he said.

14 Jul 2020

"Dear friends, this is now my second letter to you. I have written both of them as reminders to stimulate you to wholesome thinking." 2 Peter 3:1

hold on to the good

Be sure it is good before you hold on,
Before all your worth is suddenly gone—
Be sure it is worth who you are.
There always is more that seems to appeal,
A glitter of gold that serves to conceal
A nothingness, tainted, bizarre.

There always will be a new prophecy,
A way to see life, a philosophy
That challenges what you once knew,
But what someone else might choose to
    invent,
May not be worth half the effort they
    spent—
Just evil, a falsehood, untrue.

You're longing for good, you thirst and you
    pant,
And hear in the air a new song to chant,
But what are the lyrics about?
They claim to resolve the evils and woes,
To quench all your thirst, or so the song
    goes,
But pause just one stanza to doubt.

Is God in the mix, did he write each line,
Or is it just fake, a fantasy sign?
Be wary and give it a test:

Does it still uphold the greatest command,
To love God and man, do good in the land?
If not, then continue your quest.

16 Jul 2020

"Do not treat prophecies with contempt but test them all;
hold on to what is good, reject every kind of evil."
1 Thessalonians 5:20-22

the call

Yesterday I got the call—
Reluctantly, I go,
Not unwillingly at all,
But feeling just so-so,
As the chapter of my tale
Starts to fade, a little pale.

All the days of fancy-free
And straining to survive,
Have become a part of me—
I'm glad to be alive,
As each poem and each prose
Are my story, I suppose.

All good things must have an end,
But this is just the start—
Life persists, I comprehend
And persevere with heart,
Mid-pandemic, feeling strong,
Ready for another song.

And as I go back to serve
And walk across the stage,
Life is more than I deserve
As God writes every page,
So I'll go and seize the day—
There could be no other way.

18 Jul 2020

The pandemic has not passed, but I have been summoned back to work, wistful about leaving this spring and summer interlude, while persevering as life persists.

a satisfied exhale

What does it take to feel satisfied?
What does it take to be justified
In some sort of gentle exhale?
What do you feel is the missing link
Between your longings and what you think
Is just one more day that you fail?

What is fulfillment of all your dreams?
Why is it harder than what it seems
To find that elusive delight?
Somehow the worry, anxiety,
Edges into a complacency
That makes you feel nothing is right.

Talk to me, tell me what bothers you,
What is the problem you can't see through?
What is the obscure, looming cloud?
Why do you wallow without a smile,
And think that nothing is worth the while?
It might help to say it out loud.

Is at the bottom of what you fear,
Just staying stuck in this atmosphere
Where nothing like hope lingers long?
Sit back, exhale and take heart again,
Finding the hope that there was back then,
In God's love right here all along.

31 Jul 2020

It saddens me when I see someone struggle to find satisfaction, and I want to hold out some hope for them to grasp, in God.

loving intently

Don't look at me with starry
Eyes,
And plead for grace with sorry
Cries—
Your "sorry" is a waste.
You had a choice of doing
Right,
Not knowing that the ending
Might
Have such a sour taste.

So think before you say or
Do,
And find it will be best for
You,
With love and with intent,
And then our love will always
Be
A joy, a joy, and someday
See
The love that this all meant.

1 Aug 2020

In any loving relationship, it is better to do right from the
start than to regret it later and say sorry.

successful love

What is success
Without the fame,
When none can guess
Your middle name,
When all you've done
Is so obscure?
Have you begun?
I'm not so sure.

Where did you see
Your name in print?
Don't look at me—
I saw no hint
Of fame, of news,
For all to hear,
Instead I choose
To make this clear:

Your name is penned
There in the book,
And in the end,
Our God will look
And know the way
Your love was true—
Then he will say,
"I welcome you!"

2 Aug 2020

For my parents' anniversary, I bought a congratulations card that beamed about shining success, and it prompted me to ponder the best definition of success.

baby bird

Have you heard?
Baby bird
Just fell from the sky,
From the air,
Over there—
I want to know why.

Featherless,
Motionless,
He sleeps in a heap,
Cannot sing,
And his wing
Won't stir in his sleep.

None can tell
When he fell,
None saw it—did you?
And the ground
Made no sound,
No other bird knew.

Overhead,
God once said,
He sees every flight,
And he still
Does his will,
And it is just right.

There is worth
On the earth,
From high up above,
For I see
Gravity
Is held in his love.

7 Aug 2020

"Are not two sparrows sold for a penny? Yet not one of them will fall to the ground outside of your Father's care."
Matthew 10:29

plan b

So, what is plan B?
No, don't look at me—
I don't feel like thinking that much.
I just know plan A
Is starting to fray
And seems to be losing its touch.

Let's pivot and spin
And turn, rebegin,
And do it without losing heart.
The old and the new
Will blend, then: Take Two,
Without ever falling apart.

But not at all cost—
Our love can't be lost,
The reason that all this began.
Oh, God, guide us now
And help us somehow
To love only you as we plan.

21 Aug 2020

Someone came to me, saying that they had awakened
early the previous morning with a strong sense from
God that they needed to have a plan B to adapt to these
uncertain times.

love is love

Love is love, a lilting line
The butterflies might sing,
And if all the stars align,
It shines on everything.
Love is love, a blissful thought,
But it doesn't mean a lot.

Black is black, and white is white,
And grey is in between,
And when all is good and right,
Each color is unseen.
So they say, but I don't know
If that thought is apropos.

On this planet, man is man,
And woman has her place,
And some do the best they can
To merge them and erase
What love is and twist the facts—
All you butterflies, relax.

Where is God in all of this,
The one who made it all:
Butterflies in lilting bliss
And stars that sometimes fall,
Black and white and grey and brown,
Man and woman, king and clown?

God is love, and God is real—
When will we understand
What we think and how we feel
Are less than his command
To love God and let him be
God of love and mystery?

2 Sep 2020

On the heels of the BLM movement, I saw a sign in a yard stating, "We believe black lives matter, no human is illegal, love is love, women's rights are human rights, science is real, water is life, injustice anywhere is a threat to justice everywhere." While there are some truths here, it seems to lack a sense of God's identity. God is love and so much more!

wellspring of life

Oh, wellspring of life, oh, fountain of youth,
So how have we lasted this long?
We sway with our whims, becoming
    uncouth,
An aimless and mannerless throng.

We claim to stand tall and want to age well,
So no one will question our age—
Plus, what is the point of Heaven and Hell,
Since all of the world is a stage?

Be free, live it up, be strong, seize the day,
And do it the best that you can,
Then when you are done, repeat and push
    play,
And if you're that good, I'm your fan.

But back to the point of all that you do—
There must be a motive of course—
Take heed, guard your heart—it's beating
    for you,
And let only love be your source.

11 Sep 2020

"Above all else, guard your heart, for everything you do
flows from it." Proverbs 4:23

being something

Don't think that I am something
That I'm not,
Like boasting, posing, scheming
My own plot—
The happy ending isn't my own fame,
A string of letters that became my name.

I write as if each word were
A lifeline,
But life is wholly other
By design,
And I'm a being more than this despite
The value that I put in what I write.

I'm only here because God
Made me so,
And if I seem a bit odd,
I don't know—
I simply want to write and live in love,
While all the credit goes to God above.

30 Sep 2020

As a writer, I am only worth whoever God made me to be.

wanderlust

Is wanderlust a pilgrimage unheeded,
A lust for lands more pagan than divine?
But wandering is never quite completed,
And what is wanderlust without a sign?
So, then you will find when you're done
That you had just barely begun.

For wanderlust to truly be fulfilling,
The destination means more than the quest.
Our thirst for pure adventure is instilling
An aimlessness that leaves us second best,
And since there is never an end,
We search, but we don't comprehend.

But wanderlust can lead us where we're
    going,
As long as God is going with us too,
And, fearless, our adventure is in knowing
That somewhere we will get a better view
That makes all the wanderlust seem
A pilgrimage more than a dream.

9 Oct 2020

Wanderlust is misdirected when we wander without God.

being me

It's just another day of being me.
Don't ask me what that means—I'm not so
    sure.
I only know that what I'm meant to be
Is something that will linger and endure.

I'm only human—that I know full well,
But God created me and gave me breath.
And even in this poem I can tell
That life is more than birth that ends in
    death.

And even though today is just a day,
There's something more eternal in this
    rhyme,
So may my rhythm, everything I say
Be something God can craft and make
    sublime.

17 Oct 2020

I am only me, only human, but God can make something
bigger out of all of this.

the portuguese poet

They say they saw a foreign side of me,
Concealed beneath my English fluency,
And when they heard me speak in
    Portuguese,
They sensed a poet's spirit no one sees,
Like waves that speak the language of the
    shore,
A surging rhythm coming from my core.
They listened to a word so strange,
    saudade,
A longing for some something that seems
    odd,
And when I yearned with *fado*, fateful song,
They wondered if they'd known me all
    along.
What is this song, this melancholic ache,
These words like waves that give more than
    they take,
This poet who is smiling from her soul,
Who seems to be divided but so whole?
I answer them, "Just hear me one more
    time:
The oceans hide a deep, delightful rhyme."

23 Oct 2020

When I performed my Portuguese poetry via Instagram
Live as part of the 5[Th] Poetry Festival of Lisboa, Portugal,

many of my friends in the U.S.A. who only speak English also tuned into the session. Afterward, they commented that even though they did not understand the language, they were fascinated to see "another Lisa" whom they felt they had never met. What they observed was the spirit of someone who lives in the foreign land of the U.S.A. as an immigrant, navigating the local language fluidly while singing a song from across the sea.

seed by seed

Seed and seed and seed,
My fingers pluck each one.
Slowly they concede
And fall apart, undone,
Garnet beauties, sweet and tart,
Deconstructed work of art.

And I wonder why
Your beauty is concealed,
As my fingers pry
For more to be revealed.
Ruby goodness, speak, confide,
Why such grandeur deep inside?

Truly, what I seek
Is something you don't know.
Only God can speak
Of glory here below,
And in this luscious red I see
His beauty and his mystery.

Pomegranate bliss
Is worthy of the quest,
And I'm sure of this:
A goodness better, best
Is the one I soon will taste,
Seed by seed with hope, not haste.

15 Nov 2020

While plucking the seeds from a pomegranate, I pondered. Why is something that is so good for us so seemingly out of reach?

more than a whim

I thought I knew who I might be,
But it was just a whim,
And now I'm not, but I'm here, free,
Because, because of him.

My whim was like an airy mist,
That dissipates above,
And now I know, my soul is kissed
By everlasting love.

For love is not what I invent,
Like humanistic dreams,
And he has shown me life is meant
To be more than it seems.

22 Nov 2020

We think we know who we want to be, we think we know what love is, until we are truly loved. And then, we become more.

grateful destiny

Maybe being grateful
Means giving up my will,
Finding in the fateful
An ending greater still.

I am poor, created,
And cannot make a claim,
Only to be fated
To thank God, to exclaim.

Thankful to be living,
And breathing every breath,
Knowing that in giving,
That life is more than death.

If my breath is hoarded,
I miss who I can be,
But the thanks afforded
Is free, my destiny.

22 Nov 2020

Gratitude means receiving receptively and thanking freely.

vibrant simplicity

Vibrant simplicity sounds good to me,
But I suspect that it's wrong.
Life is complex, like I know it to be,
Not a naïve, happy song.
All the vibration is hurting my head,
Pulsing and pounding like torture instead.

And then you look at me, saying there's
    more.
You seem to thrive, not just cope,
And with a stillness that comes from your
    core,
You sing of some endless hope.
There is a vibrancy when you are still.
Will you explain it? Please tell me you will.

You see the beauty when I see the bruise.
You trust the end from the start,
Claiming you simply let God be your muse,
Guiding the beat of your heart.
Vibrant simplicity, two words that say:
Love everlasting. I want that today.

5 Dec 2020

Vibrant simplicity is not naïve poetic happiness. It is a life of
pure love that surges forward forever.

whole rest

And then I sketched a rest,
A block of black,
As if I could attest
To some great lack,
When really all I want and need to know
Is that I am allowed to be here, slow.

And when I recommence
To sing my song,
The rest that brought suspense
Will come along,
And touch each lyric with a note of poise,
For otherwise my song is only noise.

But more than anything
In my technique,
Each lyric that I sing
Is most unique,
When God commands the tempo of my art,
While filling up my song, just as my heart.

13 Dec 2020

The pause of a musical rest brings the promise of
more goodness afterward, particularly when all of it is
orchestrated by God.

winter solstice

The sun shows up late and then leaves in a
    sprint,
Indifferent, cold-shouldered, unkind,
Or maybe its shadows hide some lovely hint
Of wonder, of light for the blind,
A light that is hopeful, and we will soon
    peer,
To look in broad daylight, when life
    becomes clear.

The shadows that lengthen are telling a tale
Of planets and stars and of time,
And sunlight that dwindles, that dims,
    sunken, pale,
Is prodding our spirits to climb,
With hope that this winter will soon become
    spring,
And light will shine boldly upon everything.

So, let us not wallow and grope in the dark,
Lamenting the lack of the sun,
For if we look upward, an infinite spark
Is fervently there since day one:
The God of all ages, who knows every star,
Is never far from us, right here where we
    are.

21 Dec 2020

Winter solstice may seem sorrowfully dismal, but there is splendorous, wondrous delight in the God who placed every star and is ever present.

red sky

Red sky in the morning,
Sailors, take warning,
And all you poets, arise.
Keep your posture steady
And parchment ready,
While contemplating the skies.

When the night is ruddy,
Maintain your study—
Be most unswerving at night,
Like a hopeful poet,
Then you will know it:
After the dark comes delight.

28 Dec 2020

Each red sky that I see on the horizon can spark anxiety
or awe. I choose awe. I chose to be ready, be hopeful and
seek God above all else.